T0267733

THE
SMART
AND THE
DUMB

ADVANCE PRAISE FOR THE BOOK

'*The Smart and the Dumb* is a powerful critique of contemporary Indian education that exposes a stark paradox: while more people than ever seek education's empowering potential, opportunities for marginalized groups are shrinking. Through vivid stories from his journey across India, Vishal guides us through this complex landscape, revealing the disconnect between promise and reality, shedding light on hidden mechanisms that perpetuate disadvantage and questioning the fairness and effectiveness of existing systems. This powerful and thought-provoking read will spark critical conversations about education for real empowerment. A must-read for policymakers, educators and anyone concerned about building a more equitable society'—Thamizhachi Thangapandian, member of Parliament, South Chennai, Lok Sabha

'By seamlessly blending storytelling and analysis, Vishal gently compels the reader to review their opinions about the formal education system and challenges assumptions about such things as success and merit. Quietly persuasive in its approach and remarkably humane in the telling, *The Smart and the Dumb* confronts the most fundamental questions about education—the purpose it serves and the needs it meets. Above everything else, this book on education is just that—an education'—Mukund Padmanabhan, former editor, *The Hindu*

'*The Smart and the Dumb* is a probing book on Indian education—on both its promise and its unevenness. Indian schools are as diverse as India itself, and Vishal Vasanthakumar writes with compassion and care about the challenges that both students and educators face across the country. His book will be an essential primer for anyone looking to rethink the basics of how children learn in India'—Samanth Subramanian, author and journalist

THE
SMART
AND THE
DUMB

THE POLITICS OF
EDUCATION IN INDIA

VISHAL VASANTHAKUMAR

PENGUIN
VIKING
An imprint of Penguin Random House

VIKING

Viking is an imprint of the Penguin Random House group of companies
whose addresses can be found at global.penguinrandomhouse.com

Published by Penguin Random House India Pvt. Ltd
4th Floor, Capital Tower 1, MG Road,
Gurugram 122 002, Haryana, India

First published in Viking by Penguin Random House India 2024

Copyright © Vishal Vasanthakumar 2024

10 9 8 7 6 5 4 3 2

ISBN 9780670098637

Typeset in Garamond by MAP Systems, Bengaluru, India
Printed at Replika Press Pvt. Ltd, India

www.penguin.co.in

For Dr Houman Harouni

Contents

Introduction

I didn't particularly enjoy going to school, but soon after I became a teacher, a sight that captivated me was the image of children reaching school early in the morning, all arriving at the same time. More importantly, I would pay keen attention to the faces of parents. There was always so much hope and so many dreams enmeshed in that act of dropping a child off at school every morning. A congregation of young students, mostly all at the same time, radiating hope for a better future, and this was the one place where we could see dreams materialize.

Through my travels for this book, I often found myself in different schools across the country, standing by the gate early in the morning, trying to understand the dreams and aspirations with which these students were brought to school. I found myself chatting with multiple parents, some who dropped their children off in pushcarts and some who dropped their children off in BMWs. Their dreams were similar in nature, a hope for a better future, to be more 'successful' than the previous generation, to make a better life for themselves. It is what formal schooling promised: a method to access dreams that were once out of reach. But in writing this book, I began questioning whether this promise holds true.

We are all affected by globalization. I use the term 'globalization' liberally, aware that the term is laden with many assumptions and ideas taken for granted, often as self-evident truths. We live in a very interconnected world where messages can be exchanged in a second, but walls and borders are built to keep people apart. Globalization was meant to benefit everyone and integrate everyone into a global economy. However, there is sufficient evidence to suggest that globalization and the forces of globalization have contributed to new dimensions of inequality and stratification, which have implications not just for education but for politics and culture too.[1]

My grandmother always asked me to take my studies seriously, something I could not do in school. When my performance in school was poor, she often talked to me about how studying well was the only way forward. 'Don't you want to score good marks, get a good job and earn lots of money?' I remember her asking me even as I sobbed after yet another underwhelming performance. It was something I heard repeatedly from my parents and my schoolteachers too. Growing up, this was my world. My grandmother subliminally instilled in me that if one scored well, it was a reflection of one's intellect and skills, and that would lead to a high-paying job. That was the promise of formal education. But it was not just a way to earn more, it was also a route to dignity. Schooling and, by extension, education, was an investment in skills, an investment to make one more employable and a signal of one's productivity.

In India, almost every child enrols in primary school today. This is evidenced by most states' gross enrollment ratios (GER) for primary schools being at 99 or 100 per cent.[2] Thus, formal education is now a commonly shared experience for many of us, and a school is one of the most commonly found institutions not just in India but worldwide. We have all been through it and perceive the world through the lenses acquired through our years of formal schooling. But as Stephen Ball, a sociologist of education, suggests, in the wake of globalization, education is being reconceived, and what it means to be educated is changing as a result. It is being tied ever more tightly to the needs of economic competition and the knowledge economy.[3]

'Knowledge economy' is a term that didn't exist until very recently. It is a practice where production and services are based on knowledge-intensive activities that contribute to an accelerated pace of technical and scientific advancement. The key component of a knowledge economy is a greater reliance on intellectual capabilities than physical inputs or natural resources.[4] The World Bank has phrased it this way: 'A knowledge-based economy relies primarily on the use of ideas rather than physical abilities and on the application of technology . . . Equipping people to deal with these demands requires a new model of education and training.'[5] But what about the ones that continue to rely on their physical abilities rather than their intellectual ones? Do they deserve to be left behind?

Education is considered a panacea by many, a one-stop solution to address all of society's problems. For many, it is viewed as an opportunity to get out of their current way of life and seek a better future. Education is the solution to assimilate people migrating from villages to cities. In a time when old occupations are disappearing and new ones are being invented every day (for some time, I had a job as a political consultant, a term that was perhaps created a few years ago), education is supposed to help people catch up with the times. It is considered an engine for mobility, a leveller of the playing field of life, a chance for people to broaden their horizons, allowing them to take part in a constantly evolving world.

However, at the same time, education (more specifically, educational institutions) can be a tremendous gatekeeping institution. Based on the quality of education a person receives, their employment and material income standards differ. It creates the very structures that we seek to bring down. Moreover, it is deeply political, for someone has to decide what to teach, and in that act, a world is created, and disentangling from that world is often painful. There is more to education than simply rote learning, gaining skills and getting a job—something I didn't know when I was in school. But what is that 'more'? Who gets to decide it?

Globalization and formal education today have established themselves as self-evident processes, as unquestionable truths and perhaps even an act of God itself. The benefits of this process that were supposed to be for all have not been realized for a majority; a privileged few continue to corner it. When this unquestionable truth of globalization reaches the brick wall of lived realities, either the truth or the reality comes into question. It is this questioning that this book seeks to do. Our understanding of processes has been dominated by a discourse that lacks space to accommodate alternate realities. But it is also in the nature of self-evident truths to conceal their contradictions. For several decades, we, the beneficiaries of globalization, created a global dream everyone could relate to but very few could share.

In this book, I have tried to document some stories of what this 'more to education' is and how closely people's caste, class and gender are tied to it. This book has seven stories: of why a grandmother decided to get her fifteen-year-old granddaughter married to a seventeen-year-old truck driver in rural Rajasthan; of the many kids who want guns for Christmas and the psychological trauma of multilayered conflict in Manipur; of how a ban on tapping toddy from palmyra trees is affecting educational choices in Tamil Nadu; of how a mother of a child with attention-deficit/hyperactivity disorder (ADHD) has to deal with an unsupportive husband while grasping with what makes ADHD 'real'; of how many students have to write entrance exams to enter institutes that coach for entrance exams; of how students of elite private schools in Chennai take part in a series of exclusive literary events and thereby create a 'casteless' self; and of a journey of writing a history textbook for school students.

This book is written against the backdrop of increasing privatization, modernization and complexity in Indian society and the world. In such continuously changing times, the rulebooks of society are also being continually rewritten. Caste, class and gender identities, once firmly entrenched in Indian society, are transforming as our society liberalizes and modernizes itself more. This is not to say that these structures no longer exist or that education has completely broken them. As many sociologists have noted, these structures are continuously transforming themselves, sometimes even recreating and reproducing themselves.

The question I used to ask my grandmother as an angry teenager informs this book as well: What's the point? Initially, that was the title of this book, wherein I approached the stories with that very question. As I received rejection after rejection from multiple publishers over two years, I received feedback that this title was too defeatist; that it immediately made one think that I meant that education was pointless. Perhaps some of those editors were right, but the question remains and is something that I believe lies at the heart of the democratic exercise and a question we often take for granted. What does education do? Whose need does it serve?

In travelling across India to delve into the politics of education, it is not my intent to offer solutions on how to solve the quagmire of India's problems in education. This is a collection of stories—a record of my travels, experiences, conversations and reflections in search of answers to these questions: What does education mean to different people, and whose needs are being met by education?

Education, I believe, should be attuned to human needs, and to assume human needs are the needs of the knowledge economy is to be misinformed. In that sense, I seek to offer a lens through which one perceives and thinks about education. But I do not claim the lens to be absolute. In the spirit of 'true' education, I invite you, the reader, to critically engage with this book, just as we ought to critically engage with education, not taking me or this work for granted. In reading these stories, it is quite possible that you will contextualize your experience of education with the characters in these stories, and that, I believe, is essential. For in our reflective reading and understanding of the world, we will be able to 'name the world' (to borrow from Paulo Freire).[6] And in naming the world, that is to become active participants in our own education and not just learn about the world but critically engage with it, we will perhaps be able to create a better world and not take the one we have for granted.

People often conflate education with schooling. Often, the first image that comes to a person's mind when the word education comes up is a school. While a school is a primary instrument of a good education, it certainly is not the only instrument. In some of the stories, the school takes prominence, and in some, the school is hardly spoken about. Through these stories, I attempt to paint a portrait of the cultural and political processes that affect education and how education affects cultural and political processes. It is an attempt to depict the nuances that affect education and what people think about it because education cannot be seen in a vacuum, nor can it be seen just as a process of going to school. Given the political and cultural processes that largely affect and get affected by education, I hope these stories make the reader question how we are and, often, are not critical consumers of our education, not just in terms of content but also in terms of process.

Chapter 1

'The Girl Will Get Away'

'The pleasure in complete domination over another person (or other animate creature) is the very essence of the sadistic drive. Another way of formulating the same thought is to say that the aim of sadism is to transform a person into a thing, something animate into something inanimate, since by complete and absolute control the living loses one essential quality of life—freedom.'

—Eric Fromm[1]

To a weary traveller on a hot day, I can imagine that rural western Rajasthan could feel like the edge of the world or even an out-of-planet experience. Everywhere you look, it is brown. The drive from Kishangarh, a town just a few hours away from Jaipur, to Kotdi was all brown, and I was told that the summer was white-hot, and temperatures could reach up to 50 degrees Celsius, but I was there in February, when the days were hot but bearably so and the evenings cool. The railway station at Kishangarh was new and renovated, with a huge front entrance, wide roads leading to the entrance and the building itself containing various motifs of 'Rajasthani' architecture including *chattris*, decorative triangular arches and domes, while the landscape was barren, flat and brown just a few kilometres outside. Greenery and vegetation were sparse as I drove further into the arid, hot desert. It did feel like the edge of the world, or even a tottering abyss, for nothing appeared to grow, and the colours were varying shades of brown.

The road towards Kotdi, a small sleepy village inside the district of Ajmer, Rajasthan, was almost overwhelmed by thick heaps of dry, hot sand on everything. To the right of the road was more sand, and to the left, even more. But the people in Rajasthan had found a way to deal with the monotony of the landscape and its hues—by dressing up in complete contrast. I was in a shared jeep, a massive vehicle with no doors and seats to fit six to seven people at best but with at least fourteen people crammed together, all dressed in the brightest of colours. The men in the jeep were in white kurtas that fell below their knees and white pyjamas, but they wore the most colourful turbans, ranging from bright yellow and orange to some with green polka dots. The women were far more colourful wearing sarees in shades of bright reds, blues and greens, with the *pallu* of the saree pulled over their heads. I couldn't help but notice their large earrings, some made in gold. I sat in that jeep in a navy green T-shirt and black jeans, which by now were turning brown, thanks to the dust.

Kotdi is a small village with little more than a road, a few shops, a post office and tiny lanes with mostly brick houses. It also had a small fort, now mostly in ruins, which no one could tell me dated back to which era or king. It just stood there and had moulded itself into the terrain, with some wild shrubs growing over and into it. Only later did I understand that this was a common theme. Like the fort, ideas, beliefs and institutions just existed and moulded themselves into the terrain. People accepted them to be a fact of the world, a self-evident truth, a necessity for the functioning of life.

Punaramji dressed in typical fashion—a white kurta-pyjama and bright yellow turban. He was very much part of the social fabric of Kotdi, and people greeted him everywhere he went but never said anything beyond a greeting. Social hierarchies, especially that of being a Dalit man in a highly hierarchical society, had prevented him from accessing education, which he kept bringing up in our conversations. Now, he worked with an NGO called Manthan, which worked on water, education, health and livelihood issues in the surrounding areas. During my time at Kotdi, Punaramji took me everywhere he went, sometimes enthusiastically going out of his way to take me to a hamlet or a site where he had built water tanks, and I was happy to tag along. The NGO he worked for, Manthan, was widely respected and appreciated for their work in providing basic necessities, especially access to water. According to Punaramji, they had helped construct more than 200 water tanks in the district, an essential and life-changing activity in a region where water was scarce.

The more time I spent in Kotdi, where the cool evenings of February often inspired me to take long walks, often with Punaramji for company, the more stares I got. 'Are they looking at me like that because I am from out of town?' I asked one day after the staring became a bit obvious. 'No, no, you are walking with me, that's why,' he replied with a smirk. '*Mein Dalit hoon na!* (I am a Dalit),' he said and smirked again.

Punaramji certainly seemed older than fifty, though I never asked him. His hair and moustache were all grey, and he had worked with this NGO for almost twenty years. His age had given him the licence to be insightful with authority. Also, he had found credible employment in Manthan, when social hierarchies and lack of access to education had prevented him from doing much else.

Punaramji often took me to the settlements of the Bagarias —a tribal, nomadic, herding community, as he was overseeing the construction of water tanks there.

'These Bagarias are extremely poor and barely literate. Until a few years ago, they didn't even have electricity. They are nomads, you see. How could the government have cared for them if they kept moving regularly?' he said matter-of-factly as we were on our way to a settlement where the Bagarias lived. 'They keep moving. No village would typically offer them shelter, so they mostly keep to themselves.' As we continued towards the settlement, other smaller settlements appeared. '*Yahaan sab doosre jaat rehte hain* (Other castes live here),' Punaramji pointed out. These houses were all concrete. 'Do the Bagarias live here as well?' I asked. 'No, no, how will they stay here? No one will let them in,' Punaramji replied, his voice betraying a slight sense of resignation.

For centuries, the Bagarias, a tribal, herding community, have lived a semi-nomadic lifestyle. They made a living grazing the few animals they possessed, mainly cows, buffaloes and goats, and then selling the animals for meat, a profession they had been practising for generations. They also hunted for food and occasionally guarded other people's fields. Almost all government assistance seems to have missed them. Most of them didn't have birth certificates as they had never been to a hospital, and hence their children couldn't get admission to schools. They didn't have ration cards to access the free grains and oil that the government provided. They barely had any land to call their own; in any case, it was all sand. Nothing much could grow there. None of their houses had electricity or running water. In the deserts of Rajasthan, that was a nightmare.

As soon as we entered the Bagaria settlement, Punaramji exited the car and greeted a few people. '*Kaun hai ye babu*? (Who is this sir?),' asked a man pointing to me. The word 'babu' often carried a connotation of a government official, one who has authority over people's lives. It was evident that I wasn't from there, and my lack of facial hair, a closely cropped haircut and the sports shoes I wore that day were clear markers of my inhabiting a different world. The settlement was bare—there were a few mud-baked and concrete houses. Little children ran around naked, their hair and faces covered in fine coatings of sand. At the far end stood an old woman, dressed brightly in contrast with the bleak landscape, smoking a beedi. She wore a bright blue shirt with colourful orange stars, a dark green skirt with flower motifs and a bright red cloth to cover her hair. She nonchalantly looked at Punaramji as he adjusted his turban and exited the jeep. '*Aao, ji, aao,*' she said, welcoming him and me, while a young girl who didn't seem older than fifteen, slouched over a makeshift stove.

Punaramji was always a welcome figure in this Bagaria settlement. He had, as I had learnt, spearheaded an initiative to construct water tanks inside the settlement, saving Bagaria women and children the harrowing effort of walking a few kilometres to fetch a pot of water. 'How will they study if they don't even have water?' murmured Punaramji silently, as he folded his hands in a namaste to the old woman.

'Come, come. Sit. Can I get you some water?' asked the old woman.

'No, no, I am fine. I have just come to see how the water tanks are coming along,' replied Punaramji.

He looked around and noticed the many young girls slouched over those makeshift stoves outside their houses trying to light the firewood. 'Obviously, they are going to fall sick blowing smoke continuously,' he muttered to himself again and again.

'How old are these girls?' he asked a man called Kannaram who was standing beside him. I learnt Kannaram's name much later when Punaramji told me about him on our drive back. Every narration of Punaramji—of people, of locations, of stories—was all matter of fact, often bereft of any emotion. I often wondered how Punaramji adopted this stoic approach, and I reconciled myself by thinking that this was how he looked at the world. I did ask him once about his narrations and why he spoke to me this way. His reply was a simple, 'How else do I say it?'

Kannaram was the head of a family with four daughters, all within the 'marriable' age, and according to Punaramji, he was under pressure to get them married. His oldest daughter was sixteen.

Kannaram wore the look of a man saddled by a thousand responsibilities. His eyes were small and sharp and his face wore a worried expression. He worked as a labourer and went whenever and wherever there was work in someone else's field or some construction site. On the days he didn't have work, he'd sit back in his settlement, watching the day go by.

Punaramji told me that child marriage was the norm amongst the Bagarias and that he hadn't come across anyone within the community who had gotten a 'late' marriage. He seemed to accept the norm, not because he particularly supported it, but because it existed as a reality, an enduring truth of everyday life for the Bagarias.

Child marriage was commonplace in these parts. Early pregnancies were also common, even accepted. In these times, the girl was deified as a goddess, a bearer of life and perhaps not much else. 'What will a girl do by staying here, sir? It is not safe for her. People keep talking and making judgements. No family would want to take her in after a point. Another reason it happens early is if the girl grows up, some other man might take her, so we get her married early to protect her,' said Kannaram wistfully, as if he had accepted this practice as a rite of passage, something that everyone must go through.

Punaramji's presence made Kannaram defensive. Punaramji had an air of authority around this settlement. He had, after all, gotten them access to water at their doorstep. 'We get them married now but send them later,' Kannaram frowned. 'They do work after marriage. They take care of the goats or sometimes work as agricultural labourers.'

Kannaram invited us to sit and pointed to the porch of the night school built by Punaramji's organization, indicating where we could continue this conversation. Night schools were a popular concept in these regions. The children had to tend to their goats or cattle in the morning or help their parents with labour; hence, schools would start by 4 p.m. and go on till 8 p.m. We were in this settlement right when the night school started, around 4.15 p.m. Punaramji didn't want to travel in the afternoon sun, and I didn't complain. The night school was a one-room building with one teacher from a nearby village who was paid a meagre salary by a local NGO to take classes for children. He played multiple roles—school administrator, math and Hindi teacher. Kannaram and the old woman sat on the school porch while we stood at a distance, worried that we would disturb the class inside. But they didn't seem worried at all.

The old woman had now finished her beedi and lit another one. I couldn't help but notice the apparent irony, of an older woman in a deeply patriarchal society having the 'authority' to smoke around a group of men and take part in the conversation unhindered. It's like the rules didn't exist for her. She walked along with us and sat down.

'How do you get married here?' I finally asked the group, having silently observed and been observed for a while. I often worried that my questions would be naive or offensive, but Punaramji kept encouraging me to ask whatever I wanted to know. 'Sir, here our customs are quite different,' Kannaram continued with a hint of pride in his voice. 'The boy's side has to give the girl's side money, around Rs 30,000 to 40,000. This is like a price they pay for our girls. There is no concept of dowry here. The older they get, the lesser the boy's family pays us.' Only Kannaram spoke; the others silently hung on to his word. By now, there was a small group assembled around us: some other men from the settlement, some younger women and the old woman.

'Do you give gold?' I asked naively, seeking to continue the conversation.

Gold was a staple in every Indian wedding I had attended in South India, and the Indian fetish for gold has been well documented. Kannaram was excited to share by now.

'Yes, there is gold involved. But the boy's side has to do it. They give Rs 30,000 to 50,000 to the girl's parents. If the girl doesn't settle well in that house or runs away, they come to ask us for another girl from the family.' His words seemed to indicate that the woman had no agency in this. Yet, somehow, the old woman could light beedi after beedi. Paying the bride's family to bring the bride home was a method to usurp her of her agency and keep her obligated. By now, Kannaram was in his element. 'We find prospective boys or girls from neighbouring villages. And, sir, if people don't like the boy or the girl, they can say so. We will cancel it. But the way it works here is that if I am giving you a boy, you also have to give me a boy from somewhere. It's only fair, no?'

'Think of what these girls must be feeling,' whispered Punaramji, indicating for the first time in all my interactions with him a hint of emotion, pointing to a group of brightly clad young women winnowing some wheat.

'What if one of your girls says they want to go to Ajmer or Jodhpur for work?' I quickly asked, realizing very soon that it was a naive question.

'No one says anything like that; they don't go outside,' came the quick reply from Kannaram.

The old woman had lit up another beedi and continued looking at me. Meanwhile, the night schoolteacher continued with his class inside the school. Punaramji tapped on my shoulder, indicating it was time to leave. Throughout the afternoon, the women in the village silently observed us from afar, and then they watched us go.

* * *

My days in Kotdi involved driving around to various neighbouring hamlets along with Punaramji or his colleagues. We often ensured that we were indoors by noon to avoid the heat. Mornings in

Kotdi began with the sound of bells of goats clanking as little children shepherded them into a straight line on the way to graze. The sound of bells was unmissable, especially when a hundred goats walked on the road. Then, the men emerged, adjusting their turbans, sipping tea and watching the sun fill the horizon, turning the brown landscape into a bright yellow one, and soon, you could feel the presence of the sun completely. All at once, it became hot. Then those who had work would leave, and those who didn't would idyllically watch them.

Those who were employed worked outside Kotdi, in the marble hub of Kishangarh, an hour's drive away. Life in this village was idyllic, and like the others, I soon settled into taking multiple naps as and when I felt like it. Old men sat around playing cards under the shade of a tree; some gossiped about the man who beat his wife or the girl who had run away. Others would take a nap on their charpoys.

Soon, it became impossible to walk around in the heat, and a stillness descended. Everyone retreats to some form of shade inside; a friend's shop, a godown, a hay barn, or, when possible, someone's house large enough to shelter them. But it was mostly men whom I speak about here. The women, from before dawn, prepared meals, dusted the house, did the laundry and stacked hay, and until Punaramji's organization came along, the women had to fetch water as well.

Everywhere I went, sand was dominant, and the landscape was dotted with shrubs that appeared unbothered by the heat or sand. Everywhere I went, I heard stories of girls getting married by fourteen or fifteen.

One person whose story was unusual was Nisha, who had been married at ten and divorced at fourteen, all within the small confines of the village of Kotdi. 'I enjoyed my wedding a lot,' Nisha recalled. 'I was ten and everyone told me that I looked like a little doll. Everyone around looked happy also; they told me what to do, so I did it.'

When I went to meet Nisha, she welcomed me enthusiastically, while her mother eyed me with suspicion. I had gotten to know about Nisha's story from some people who were at Punaramji's NGO, which was running night schools. Nisha was a product of the night school, having done most of her schooling there, and now was doing a bachelor's in botany. Nisha didn't go to school initially. She grazed and watched over goats. 'My mother used to work in the salt fields, so someone had to take care of the goats,' she said, carrying a bundle of hay and putting it in the shed. The night school provided her an opportunity to experience education for the first time at the age of six.

'But the night school really helped; I could graze the goats and then go to school too,' she continued. 'There were many days when I would lose track of some of the goats, and I would be late to school, but no one scolded me at the night school. They all understood.' Nisha was happy in school; she felt like she belonged there and enjoyed the environment of the school, during twilight and after dark. It gave her a sense of possibility that there is more to the world than Kotdi, the very thing the elders in Kotdi feared.

And then Nisha got married; she was ten. The boy was from the neighbouring village; he was twelve. Her paternal uncle's son was getting married at a relatively more respectable age of sixteen. 'Why spend separately on two weddings?' Nisha laughed. 'When he got married, they got me married as well.'

The concept of choice didn't seem to exist. Children were to do what their parents asked of them, and then the cycle repeated itself, generation after generation. Nisha's uncle had committed her to a circle of certainty, her reality seemingly imprisoned. Her family made up their own truths. '*Beta*, you are protecting our family's honour.' 'Good girls get married early.' 'You will be happy!' This was what Nisha was told by her uncle. In committing to this circle of certainty, Nisha's family were conditioned by the contradictions of their reality. Soon enough, these girls, married quite early, would go on to become mothers and would want their children to get married early as well. In Paulo Freire's words, 'they had adopted an attitude of adhesion to the oppressor'.[2]

Perhaps Nisha's family feared freedom. 'Everything is decided by the elders; no one cares about your intentions, what you like, what you want, whether you are actually fit for marriage,' she said.

In any case, Nisha was married. Tradition in Kotdi didn't allow for the bride to go to her in-laws' place until she was at least fifteen or had achieved puberty. Nisha finished her wedding rituals, and later that night, she returned home to continue grazing her goats by the day and going to school at night.

A little after a year after she got married, a drought hit Kotdi. Nisha would often miss school, for she had to fetch water and graze the goats, and these activities took time. 'I had to go collect water from quite far off, and by the time I could finish grazing the goats and getting water, I was exhausted. I just couldn't go to school.'

One morning, four men arrived at Nisha's house with spades and began digging a ditch inside the courtyard of her house. One of them was Punaramji, accompanied by people from his NGO. They were building a water tank that a tanker lorry carrying potable drinking water would fill up. Soon enough, Nisha didn't have to walk miles under the hot desert sun to get water. She could go to school. When the quality of education is good, people soon start getting options, an ability to choose. But to be able to choose, Nisha needed the option of water near her own home. For her, access to education hinged on the possibility of having that option.

But this was short-lived. She was a good student, but she was fourteen and married, honour bound to move in with her husband and in-laws. The in-laws had started calling, asking when her parents would send Nisha over. It meant starting a whole new life, away from the comforts of her home, away from her goats and her friends down the street. It meant taking care of her husband, a man she had seen once when she was ten, her in-laws and their house. It meant stopping going to school. 'They said when I went there, they wouldn't let me study,' she said grimly. 'What is she going to do by studying, was their question.'

What promise did schooling hold? Nisha's mother and in-laws were scared that *ladki haath se chhut jayegi* (the girl will get away or out of hand).

Those in Kotdi who went to school studied till Class 8, but they could barely write their name or perform three-digit subtractions. But this was not a situation limited to Kotdi. It was a phenomenon across Rajasthan and even India. According to the Annual Survey of Education Report 2022, only 17.32 per cent of all kids in Class 5 in Rajasthan could perform subtraction.[3] The only option for a real education was a private school, 40 kilometres away in the town of Roopangarh, which charged a fee of about Rs 30,000 a year, a sum unimaginable to Nisha's mother and undoubtedly preposterous for Nisha's in-laws. The very notion of a young married girl living alone in a town was beyond imagination. When something is beyond imagination, it is usually quickly dismissed as scandalous or heresy.

'I don't want to go, Ma, please don't send me there. I want to study, I will study well,' Nisha cried and cried. She lay in her room for days, refusing to eat, tears flowing from her eyes. Her eyes were puffy and red from all the crying, and a lingering feeling of hopelessness hung in the dry desert air. Her tears fell to the ground and in a few seconds, the spots where the teardrops fell disappeared. This land seemed to be as unforgiving as her reality.

'We'll work it out,' Nisha's mother promised. But Nisha was having nothing of it. Grazing goats during the day had given Nisha enough time to reflect and build a resolve. The night school had shown her other worlds; it transported her into imaginary realms far outside this unforgiving land in which tears, dreams and hopes quickly disappeared. 'I saw that my teachers were older than me, and some were not married,' she said. Nisha was firm that she was not going to go to her in-laws.

Some of her neighbours belonging to the dominant upper caste and having access to social networks and economic opportunities had been able to pursue some education and were seemingly doing well for themselves, mainly in Kishangarh. People from Nisha's school came and tried to convince her mother. As it turned out, Nisha's mother was on her side, an ally. She had decided that she would make her daughter study, moved by Nisha's sheer willpower, or perhaps she'd just had enough of the whole thing. It was a decision that took an enormous amount of courage and resolve. Her mother refused to talk to me about this; it was an ordeal she wanted to put behind her. Nisha could study now, but her mother had to face everyone else.

They told the boy's family that she was not going to come and that they were going to 'divorce' him. 'Once I had decided this, it was easy to tell them,' Nisha said. 'There was guilt that I would bring down the honour of my family, that my mother won't be able to show her face to anyone. But my mother supported me.'

The divorce was finalized, except that there was no registration of the marriage. There was no document that she could sign as she was a child when she had been married. But the verbal agreement of marriage was stronger than any state-governed contract.

'We have a system here called *Atta-Satta*. So, when I didn't go, they decided not to send a girl from their side. It all got balanced,' Nisha laughed. There wasn't an illusion of choice either. The elders, always the elderly men, decided who would get married where and in case someone 'dropped out' of getting married, they wouldn't send someone else.

'Marriage isn't a choice here. It is an inevitability,' Nisha laughed again, shooing a couple of baby goats into their enclosure. 'People don't let you work after you get married, and if you don't get married, you can't do anything.' There was a sense of humour in her voice, as if she had reconciled to her reality, and she was able to see the irony of it all.

Today, Nisha works in a local school near Kotdi. Her mother remains worried about who will marry her daughter now.

Education had given Nisha not just capabilities but the ability to choose. She decided to choose her own identity, not the one ascribed to her for being born a woman. But in a society where identities and choices are tightly controlled, building a new identity was akin to destroying established modes of thinking, those that kept the wheels of her society functional.

But Nisha's was a unique story, an outlier. Punaramji and the volunteers at Manthan pressed me not to take this as a success story that could be replicated. 'For every Nisha, we have a hundred other married girl children,' said Punaramji.

* * *

'But *Dadi*, what will you do to get her married so early? She is just fourteen, and she has a bright future in front of her. What about her studies then?' asked Sanjana confidently in Govardhanpura, Rajasthan.

Govardhanpura was not too different from Kotdi. Like Kotdi, it was also a small village located a short drive away from Kishangarh railway station. Sand was everywhere, and tall, green and thorny shrubs dotted the landscape. The state of settlements in the village indicated that there was abject poverty. There wasn't much employment, and the school in the village was run down. People made ends meet by herding goats or going to Kishangarh, the nearest town, in search of some employment.

Sanjana was a volunteer at a local NGO and had built a gender awareness curriculum to teach children about gender and sexual assault in and around the villages of Tilonia and Govardhanpura, neighbouring villages to Kotdi. A part of her job included convincing parents or caretakers not to take their children out of school. A common reason for dropping out was that the child was getting married, and Sanjana was here again to try and convince parents that it was better if they remained in school. Sanjana was a determined field worker; she had been working with the NGO and the locals long enough to know that she could not solve these problems by herself, but she also knew she had something to offer, and that once she had established a rapport with the locals, they would at least listen to what she had to say. As I did with Punaramji, I tagged along with her everywhere she went. She had asked me a day earlier if I would like to accompany her to meet this young girl dropping out of school to get married.

Sanjana entered the courtyard of Dadi's house in Govardhanpura. The house was bare; the entire property consisted of a front yard and a one-room concrete structure that functioned as a kitchen, living room and sleeping quarters. Dadi lived alone there with her granddaughter, Kusum. Their relatives were in other villages, and her uncle lived in another village close by. Dadi had one son, who had passed away a few years ago and her daughter-in-law had re-married soon after.

'What is she going to do by staying at home? I clean dishes, sweep houses and dry cow dung just so that I can feed her. Her useless father drank enough to kill himself, and her mother ran away. How much longer can I take care of her? She is fifteen; she is old enough to run a house,' answered Dadi with that cold pragmatic logic that can come when all one can think of is survival and does not have the luxury to take it for granted.

'You see the boy once, no. You will see why he is a good match,' said Dadi, beckoning to Kusum to bring a photo. Kusum giggled. She went into the house and came out with a small photograph. He was just a boy, certainly not a man yet. He had angry pimples across his face, his hair was oiled and draped across his forehead, and he had a skinny exterior.

'How old is he?' asked Sanjana.

'He's seventeen, older than Kusum.'

'What does he do?'

'He drives trucks. Big vehicle; he will take care of Kusum well.'

At that moment, the question of who gave a seventeen-year-old a truck-driving licence was beside the point.

'He's good-looking, isn't he?' chuckled Dadi, and everyone giggled.

'*Suno, beti*, all your talk about going to school is okay. Do you know how far she has to walk to that night school? More than a kilometre. All the boys leer at her when she's walking back.'

Dadi continued, 'What will happen to our honour? There will be gossip soon about how she is not yet married and walking alone at night. You can't trust the boys in this area.'

'Dadi, we will walk her to school and back. That is not a problem. She will grow up, and she will scold you,' said Sanjana, continuing the back-and-forth battle of competing rationales.

'She won't scold me and all. Ask her yourself,' laughed Dadi.

'Do you want to get married, Kusum?' asked Sanjana.

Kusum pointed to the picture. 'He is handsome,' she giggled.

'Dadi, you don't even know him. How can you trust him or his family?' asked Sanjana, realizing that the conversation was slipping out of control.

'Enough,' Dadi declared and folded her hands, signalling that the conversation was over. We had outstayed our welcome.

Sanjana shrugged, thanked Dadi for her time and left. The blushing bride-to-be and her grandmother had made their decision, and anything more was an intrusion. In a world of a thousand issues associated with being a woman in Rajasthan, being in places like Kotdi and Govardhanpura sprung a thousand more. How could education be very high on the list of priorities?

The contrast couldn't have been sharper between Nisha and Kusum. One had used education to get out of a marriage, and the other was being denied education to get into one. Nisha had divorced an older boy, and Kusum was about to marry one.

If education wasn't high on the list of priorities, the idea of choice didn't seem to be either. A wedding was a big occasion in the family, but a wedding was also a burden, especially if you had multiple girls. All they got in return from the groom's family was a bride fee, a measure of thanks for sending their girl to the groom's house. People were proud of it, of course.

A favourite pastime in India is to sit at tea shops, watch the world go by and maybe talk to the person next to you about someone else. One was bound to find colourful people and stories at these tea shops. It was never just a place to drink tea; it was a site for cultural transmission. Late one evening in Kotdi, Punaramji and I decided to take a walk, soak in the cool winter air and sip tea.

'*Arey o bhai, kaise ho*, how are you?' asked Punaramji at the sight of a familiar face. The tea shop always had familiar faces. Punaramji introduced me as a journalist, here to write stories about education. By now, people had become familiar with me. I was the boy who would walk around the village asking questions. When I first arrived, I always felt a gaze on me. It was unsettling, but soon I had gotten used to it, just like they had gotten used to me. No one had asked who I was or why I was there; they were just happy to gaze. When Punaramji introduced me, it felt like they had found the answer to their latent question. In a minute, someone had already bought me a cup of tea.

It took a while for everyone to settle down, for a barrage of questions followed as soon I was introduced. How are you sleeping here? Do you feel the lack of an AC? How many siblings do you have? What do your parents do? How do you like Kotdi? Would you like to come home for dinner? Is Punaramji treating you well? Are you married? Do you have children?

'What do you think about the idea of marriage here?' I asked once everyone had settled down after I had sufficiently answered their questions and assured them that I would be getting married sooner rather than later.

'Only here there is no dowry; the groom's family pays the bride's family,' said Ramcharan, a man in his late forties, wearing a bright red turban and all whites, sipping his tea slowly.

'What if the girl doesn't want it?' I asked out of naive curiosity.

'The girl will always want to make her parents happy, *beta*,' Ramcharan laughed, as if it were a self-evident truth. How was one to judge it was not?

'There's a wedding tomorrow; you should come. *Achcha khaana milega* (you will get good food),' said Ramcharan. Punaramji looked at me quizzically. I certainly wanted to go.

For some reason, everyone seemed comfortable sharing. Perhaps, it was the cool winter breeze setting in. I wanted to push my luck.

'What do you think of the idea of children getting married?' I asked nervously.

'See, *beta*, it shouldn't happen, but it happens. There's not much one can do about it. *Shaadi to hona hi hai na* (a wedding has to happen anyway),' Ramcharan said, lost in thought and looking in the other direction.

'We'll see you there,' I said and put my tea glass down. 'Oh, by the way, who is getting married?' I asked.

'It is a double wedding. Two brothers of one family are marrying two sisters of another family, all from Kotdi. Such a united family they are going to be,' Ramcharan replied happily.

The women were decked in their finest, the brightness of colours hitting one sharply in the eye. It was twilight the next day, and the last rays of the sun reflected brightly on the yellows and oranges worn by the women. The wedding was taking place in the house and farm of the brides' family itself.

'Why hire a hall when you have a nice big house and farm?' one attendee commented.

The entrance to the venue was under a white and purple shamiana, with the house itself completely decked up with blue and white cloths. A large group of enthusiastic young boys welcomed me as I shuffled awkwardly, unsure of what to do. Punaramji was busy in conversation elsewhere, and I was alone, in a wedding (double!) where I knew no one.

'Come, come, please eat,' these boys said, holding my arm and pointing towards a tent, the inside of which had long tables and chairs for people to sit in a line and eat. My feet moved involuntarily, for I was dragged along to the eating tent. The tent had only men, intensely focused on their plates, heads down, their turbans amplifying the size of their faces.

The women were in the neighbouring tent, groups of four huddled together on the floor eating out of one plate. No one told me why; they just shrugged their shoulders when I asked.

Soon enough, there were loud drumbeats. Some of the younger girls giggled, '*Baarat aa gaya.*' The groom's side had arrived while a band played trumpets and some drums, a saviour's welcome. The two grooms wore dashing grey and blue suits, which fit them perfectly. They came on horses, with swords and scabbards attached to their sides. Everyone cheered as they entered. The elder brother was about twenty or twenty-one; he had a sharp jawline, neatly combed hair and a beard that clung perfectly to his face. The younger brother was all of eighteen, the childishness on his visage was evident, and he certainly appeared to be enjoying the attention. He beamed happily at the crowd while taking off his turban to get off the horse. I half expected both of them to wave at the small crowd that had gathered.

In the front yard of the house lay all the gifts that they were to take home after the wedding. A brand-new car for the elder groom, a big cot and mattress for each couple, pillows, two huge cupboards with mirrors, refrigerators, chairs and food processors. The bride's family had bought enough for their daughters to build a home with their husbands. This was clearly one of the wealthier families in the village. The grooms surveyed the gifts from afar, seemingly happy with them as they entered the home. The trumpets and the drums were deafening.

The grooms and their families were quickly whisked into the tents where food was being served. The men were taken to a tent where they sat on chairs and ate off their individual plates laid out on tables, while the women were taken to a tent where they sat on the floor in small groups and ate off the same plate.

The rituals finally began; the men all huddled in the courtyard of the house and a Brahmin priest began chanting. The women were inside, heads completely covered, not allowed to come out until the priest had finished chanting.

And, then, they finally did. Decked head to toe in bright reds and yellows, heads covered, the brides walked out in front of everyone. They didn't raise their heads once and continuously held on to the cloth that covered their heads. They were made to sit next to their respective grooms. Had they seen their grooms before? I didn't know.

The rituals continued, and the brides continued to keep their heads down. The grooms were participating in the rituals, dutifully doing what they were told. I tried to sneak a look at the brides, to catch a glimpse of their faces. After what seemed like forever, they raised their heads. Beneath the cloth that covered their heads and partially their faces, I saw two shy smiles. They seemed happy.

After the rituals, Punaramji signalled that it was time to leave. We got into his car and he cranked it to start. It was pitch dark by now; the interior streets in Kotdi didn't have any streetlights. 'How old must the brides be?' I asked.

'The elder groom's wife is eighteen, and the younger groom's wife is fifteen. They will probably send the fifteen-year-old to her *sasural*, in-laws' place, after she turns seventeen or eighteen.' Punaramji seemed resigned to the happenings, but everyone else looked happy.

Punaramji continued driving, lost in his own thoughts and I in mine. There were schools in Kotdi and Govardhanpura, both government-run schools and schools run by NGOs. But that's what they were, just schools. These schools remained institutions of mechanical reproduction of knowledge, where the teacher's authority often conflicted with the family's authority. The hope that sending girls to school would solve particular issues seemed unfounded.

In Kusum's case, school didn't necessarily offer hope or open doors to an alternate reality. It, in fact, symbolized a danger to her grandmother, that if a girl was too educated, she would 'get away' or get out of hand. Where I considered schooling a way to bring honour to one's family, by obtaining specific credentials (finishing Class 12, getting a college degree, etc.), schools for some, like Kusum's grandmother, symbolized the potential to take away the family's honour. In that sense, the schools in Kotdi and Govardhanpura didn't just represent a beacon of hope or an engine for mobility. Schools were isolated victims of multiple external processes. For the brides, education didn't seem to be just going to school and learning the syllabus; it was about learning their 'positionality', who they were and what they were capable of, and it was well taught to them by their families, a 'site of education' unto itself. Brave women like Nisha offered some hope, but the struggle continued.

Chapter 2

Guns for Christmas

'The way people choose to remember an event, a history, is at least as important as what one might call the "facts" of that history, for after all, these latter are not self-evident givens; instead, they too are interpretations, as remembered or recorded by one individual or another.'

—Urvashi Butalia[1]

Manipur felt confined, a bit cramped, though it is quite large. Imphal, its capital, was a valley city surrounded on all sides by mountains. In the mountains lived various tribes, who were surrounded by more mountains and varying infrastructure with many still not having access to roads. Manipur had known violence for a very long time; it is the state with one of the longest-running insurgencies in India, an insurgency as old as independent India itself. When I arrived in Imphal in mid-2021, right when the COVID-19 pandemic was waning in India, Manipur was seeing its longest period of peace, at least relative to its violent and gory past. It felt like people were now in a tearing hurry to leave the past behind and move on and engaged in a continuous battle of what Manipur should be, what its people should aspire for, and in which direction they would go.

It was in stark contrast to the civil war-like situation that was happening in Manipur at the time of writing this chapter.

Imphal is a dusty city; as vehicles drive by, they leave behind a cloud of dust, which ultimately descends on another vehicle or people walking by. Naturally, people would want to shake it off, change into something cleaner or at least move to a cleaner spot. I often felt that people wanted to shake off a lot more than just the dust. It was now a new time, a time to reengineer the past to pave the way for a better future. It was a time of hope, of peace, and an interesting time for a journalist to arrive. It is one thing to write stories about a place during conflict, for these are stories to share and document so that the rest of the world can also know what human beings are capable of doing to each other, so that it weighs on our conscience to take collective action. But to arrive in a post-conflict zone and to intend to write about the violence of the past often felt like disturbing their hard-earned peace. But I had a sense that people didn't want to forget, not when there were naked signs and reminders of the past. In peacetime, you don't see the resentment that hides beneath the surface. Or, I suppose, one chooses not to. In some parts of the world, there are miles and miles of books in libraries documenting every war in minute detail, museums stacked with spoils, archives filled with documents. But here, even the most vicious violence was quickly forgotten. Traces of it soon vanish; a concrete home is built over a grave, and, now, roads. The dead are buried quickly, wounds quickly sutured, bones healed and new homes built over burnt ones. It was in such a space and time that I arrived in Manipur, where emotions appeared subdued, the atmosphere a little more accepting, a very different time than that of publishing this, when the resentment beneath had exploded out on the surface.

I exited Imphal airport to the sight of sand bunkers peopled by men in army fatigues, their hands on fully loaded guns and eyes ever vigilant. As my autorickshaw drove me through some of the main roads of Imphal to my accommodation near the Ima Keithel market, right in the centre of the city, I noticed many more men in army fatigues and police uniforms, all with guns. The Ima Keithel market is a sensory overload; sacks and sacks of vegetables, fruits and flowers moving around, people shouting instructions to each other, women sitting at small stalls selling flowers and chillies and on the farther end, rows and rows of shops selling clothes and sneakers. The sights and smells were, at the same time, effervescent and pungent.

Standing in the market, you wouldn't feel like anything was amiss. It was a bustling market, like you would find in any populous city in India, except that there were guns everywhere. Men in uniform, some different from those I had seen at the airport, stood around, guns in hand. These men just stood, holding fully loaded assault rifles, one finger on the trigger. Others around them went about their business, goods vehicles honked, and people yelled at others to get out of the way. I found myself confused, cramped, maybe even claustrophobic. It was an open market; it felt normal, but guns and men in uniforms were everywhere. I still couldn't articulate the dissonant feelings within.

I got off the auto and began walking to my accommodation, a quaint old house in a narrow street a little away from the market. As I walked, an army patrol vehicle drove past, a loaded gun on top and two men surveying opposite sides. The gun swivelled as the vehicle drove over a pothole, no longer pointing ahead but now directly at people. Not an eyebrow was raised. People continued going about their day; the guns didn't seem to bother them much, even as I could feel my body stiffen.

Many scholars and political commentators have noted that almost every written account of modern Manipur begins with a recital of the circumstances under which the territory lost its independent status and was merged into the Union of India.

The thrust of these accounts is that the merger of Manipur was accomplished with a combination of cajolement, promises that were not kept and plain trickery.[2]

In 1949, when over 500 princely states in India had already merged into the Indian Union, the Maharaja of Manipur was presented with an already prepared 'merger agreement'. While the Maharaja stood firm in his refusal to sign the agreement without consultation with his council of ministers, he was put under immediate house arrest and barred from any communication with the outside world. Simultaneously, in Imphal, Indian forces encircled the palace, seized control of telephone and telegraph lines and effectively isolated the Maharaja from his people. There was no referendum, no consultation with the multiple ethnic groups, each of which had very distinct cultural practices. The states of Manipur and Tripura, as we know them today, were first 'Part-C' states, a category made up of small princely states of the colonial era that became chief commissioner's provinces, and then Union Territories and finally a state of the Indian Union only in 1972. The disconnect of Manipur and indeed much of Northeast India with mainland India is an unaddressed phenomenon that goes back to 1947.[3]

I was to meet R, a lawyer born and raised in Imphal, working on an array of drug-related cases in Manipur. The sale of contraband and illicit drugs had become a multinational, multi-million-dollar trade in the state. R had brought along another friend, A. R felt it would be interesting for me to hear A's stories. This happened often throughout my time in Manipur. People volunteered to share their stories, mostly without my asking.

'We have seen so much violence here that it doesn't affect me any more,' said A, casually eating a plate of singju, a local Meitei delicacy. 'I was studying in Guwahati when the CAA/NRC protests were happening across the country. The armed forces surrounded and barricaded our campus with tanks.

No one could come in or go out. They wanted to starve the students to stop the protests. My friends from other parts of the country were freaking out, but I was unperturbed. My initial reaction was that I felt numb.' It is interesting to note that the CAA/NRC protests in Assam and other parts of Northeast India had a very different angle. In these parts, the protests against it were based on the claim that Bangladeshi Hindus would settle in Assam and other regions, thereby upsetting the fragile and sensitive political landscape of the region. It is also an indication that the concept of Northeast India was one of regional re-organization that didn't completely consider the multiplicity of ethnicities and aspirations of people in the region. The Northeast is often considered as one large social and political entity, which ultimately subsumes the multitudes of people in this region.[4]

'It's nothing new for us, of course. But every time we see someone in uniform, our bodies tighten,' R added. Anyone's body would clench when you see a stiff army man carrying a fully loaded gun, ready to shoot at the slightest provocation. But the real chill of walking past two commandos holding automatic rifles to enter my quaint little accommodation in the middle of Imphal was something I did not expect.

The conflicts in Manipur had layers upon layers to it; any one account to characterize it would run the severe risk of being reductionist or missing out on the subtle nuances of the conflicts and the multiple human narratives that ran through it. I don't really know where it began, or how. I came across different stories in different places, memories of origins warped with present trauma. But that seems to be an enduring trait of prolonged conflicts across the world. The intricacies of these conflicts and the opinion of their stakeholders ensured that the violence would not die down any time soon.

The Armed Forces (Special Powers) Act, 1958 (AFSPA), touched a particularly raw nerve. It was an act passed by the

Parliament of India to grant 'special powers' to the armed forces in areas where public disturbances were prevalent. According to AFSPA, the army could arrest people without a warrant if there was reasonable suspicion and could even open fire if they felt a person was in contravention of the law. It also granted the armed forces the licence to search private property without a warrant.[5] AFSPA had created a deep sense of resentment among the people of Manipur. There were stories aplenty about the excesses and atrocities of the Indian Army.

The story that A narrated to me was chilling. It was 3.40 a.m., sometime early on in 2010. A was fast asleep one night. Suddenly, she heard loud knocks on her front door. 'It was a group of army men, all holding guns. They ordered us to come out of our house and squat,' A recollected. 'Combing operations' like these were common during the height of the insurgency. If being asked to squat in front of your house wasn't humiliation enough, this was in peak winter, when temperatures could fall to sub-zero. The army men were apparently looking for an insurgent that A's family was hiding. 'Suddenly, we heard a noise from inside and only then did we realize that we had left my younger sister inside the house. My father realized what had happened. He got up and pleaded with the army men. They took us inside the house.'

A said what she saw next would never leave her. Seven army men were holding her little sister, all of the age of ten, at gunpoint while she was fast asleep wrapped underneath a blanket, head to toe, oblivious to what was happening. 'If she had moved even an inch, they would have shot her.'

Everyone I met had a story like this, something that had happened to them or their family members over the last fifty years. Manipur was a military state operating within the confines of the Constitution of India, and I sensed anger and helplessness about what had happened in the past. Just two days in, I was feeling uncomfortable. I couldn't articulate what it was, but going from having seen guns only in movies to seeing guns while leaving my accommodation, patrol vehicles loaded with assault rifles and vigilant men in uniforms made me feel very uncomfortable indeed. One had to walk around these regions with a purpose; you had to have a clear, concrete goal, or you would attract the suspicion of an army man or policeman. They seemed well-trained in distinguishing between the gait of someone walking with purpose, a goal, and someone loafing around with no purpose. In the dark past, the lack of a purpose in gait meant trouble, often a skirmish ending with gunshots, bloodshed and chaos. While walking, it felt like you either had to be going to work or going home from work.

In this claustrophobia, M, a Thangkul Naga and a Christian, who was living in a state deeply divided by religion and tribal and linguistic identities, was a friend I had grown to rely upon during my time in Manipur. I had reached Imphal on the invitation of M, whom I had told about the idea of this book. He asked me to come over to Imphal at the earliest and said he would help in figuring out accommodation and would also take me along in his work to border areas in Manipur. The conflict and stories here were so foreign to me that I desperately needed an insider to sort through them. I would ask him one question, and the answer would be a conversation that could go on for hours. M had the face of a young boy even though he was in his late twenties, his eyes ever glinting with enthusiasm. He had grown up through the violence, an angry kid, but had since calmed down as life and responsibilities had caught up with him. That anger had now been channelled into seemingly unlimited reservoirs of energy. M was a teacher, running an NGO and helping improve the quality of education in government schools across Manipur, especially up in the Naga hills.

'The Manorama incident really brought things to a boiling point here,' said M one day, on one of our journeys up to the Naga hills. Thangjam Manorama's mutilated body was found abandoned a short distance from her house on the outskirts of Imphal in July 2004. She had been picked up by the Assam Rifles, the dominant paramilitary battalion in Manipur, on the pretext of an interrogation, under suspicion of being an insurgent. Reports claim that her body was found with sixteen bullets in her genitals and with multiple other bullet wounds in her body.[6] An autopsy confirmed that she was raped before being killed.

'Women stripped naked and protested in front of the Assam Rifles' headquarters and asked the Indian army to rape them as well. It was something no one had ever seen before. I remember I was just a little boy at this time, and this was all everyone spoke about,' M said, continuing to look ahead as he drove, his eyes glazed as he recollected these incidents.[7] I had driven past the Assam Rifles camp a few times when I was in Imphal, its large imposing gates, with small banners and graffiti on its walls that read 'Sentinels of the North-East' and 'Friends of the hill people'.

An army's usage of women's bodies to drive home a military and political message has been well documented,[8] but this incident shook everyone's conscience. Anxiety, post-traumatic stress disorder (PTSD) and nightmares had now become part of everyday conversation in Manipur, even if people weren't particularly aware of the meaning of this jargon. The trauma of such incidents was carried into educational settings by students as well. 'I was an angry kid in school, ready to pick a fight with anybody over anything. It was only after going outside Manipur to study did I realize that this anger was a manifestation of something else. I used to have nightmares, waking up in the middle of the night thinking about the army. Even now, there are so many army outposts and army people staring at you,' M continued. 'When I was in school, my days were filled with the sound of bells suddenly ringing, announcing that there is some curfew, some bandh or some killing and that we have to go home immediately. This was during the peak of the conflict.'

As I travelled with M, every time the car passed from one settlement to another, we saw an army outpost with men in uniforms, guns at the ready, staring deep into my eyes. It was as if they were searching into my soul to see if I were an insurgent or if my eyes could betray a sense of fear that I was carrying something I shouldn't. Every time, I hoped they couldn't see the stiffness in my body while I tried to avoid eye contact. M seemed nonchalant about this and just nodded along whenever I told him what I felt after a routine stop at a check-post.

'I will be going to my village, and they stop and ask where I am going. I say I am going to my village, and they ask me why. Someone who is not even from here is asking me why I am going to my village. If you are going to Chennai, and someone from outside stops you and asks why you are going to Chennai, you would get angry, wouldn't you?' asked M. I spent many days in Manipur like this, driving from one district to another with M. He felt it was important for me to know about the history of the conflict, and our drives were filled with anecdotes and insights about the dynamics of multiple conflicts.

Imphal is a valley city inhabited predominantly by Meiteis, an ethnic group that adopted Hinduism, Buddhism and Islam besides following their indigenous tradition known as Sanamahi and who now constitute about 53 per cent of the population.[9] Surrounding Imphal on all sides are hills that have been inhabited by the Naga and Kuki tribes for hundreds of years. The Naga tribes have always insisted on their unique history and asserted that they have never identified with the Union of India. They identify themselves to be a part of Nagalim, which includes modern-day Nagaland, the hills of Manipur and parts of Arunachal Pradesh, Mizoram, Tripura and Myanmar. The incorporation of Manipur and Nagaland into the Indian Union gave rise to multiple insurgency movements with a dizzying array of agendas and complications. In Manipur, there is a dominant

Naga population in the hills to the north, west and east of the Imphal Valley, the Meitei live predominantly in Imphal, and the Zo people (also known as Kukis) live in the hills south of Imphal. The insurgent groups came up as a response to the capture of government contracts in the North-east immediately after Independence.[10] From the outset of the conflict in the 1950s, the Nagas started staking claims to different parts of Nagalim, and when they asked other ethnic groups to vacate their settlements, other insurgent groups came up.

The result was a military occupation of the state, with insurgent groups disintegrating into extortion gangs and groups with reputations to make or break elections. 'These insurgent groups decide who will win the elections,' M chuckled. 'It was once a battle between two sides—the state and the groups who opposed the state. Now, it is a battle between the army, the paramilitary, the Indian Reserve Battalion, Manipur Rifles, Manipur Police Commandos, village defence forces, militant groups funded and managed by the military, politicians and banned "terrorist" outfits.'

Over the course of my stay in Manipur, I came across an alphabet soup of insurgent groups—NSCN-IM, NSCN-K, NSCN-KK, NSCN-U, NSCN-R, NNC-NA, NNC-A, GPRN, FGN-A, UNLF, PLA and KCP.[11] The list went on. Conflicts within the state often took on ethnic, religious and linguistic dimensions as well. The Meiteis, who are predominantly Hindus, live in the Imphal Valley, which has a highly fertile land, while the Nagas and the Kukis in the hills are Christian. Beyond questions of development, which people in the valley had disproportional access to, language also played an undoubtable role in assimilation processes and oftentimes became a bone of contention. One instance of this was seen when Manipuri or Meiteilon (the language spoken by the Meiteis) was declared as Manipur's official language in 1979, triggering fears of cultural imposition among

minority groups, with multiple clashes occurring over the next
twenty years, some deadly.[12]

Different ethnic groups, the Meiteis, the Nagas and the
Kukis, have all called for independence from the Indian state at
different points in time, whilst having ethnic conflicts amongst
each other, often leading to disproportional violence meted out
by the Indian Army.

Meitei disaffection with mainland India is based on deep
historical scars. Independent Meitei kingdoms have been
known to exist for hundreds of years, with an uninterrupted
literary and linguistic tradition going back at least a thousand
years.[13] The forcible cession of Manipur (as we know it today)
notwithstanding, the Meiteis were further aggrieved when
Nagaland was granted full statehood in 1963, while the same
was denied to Manipur. This unrest soon escalated into violence
between Meitei insurgent groups and the Indian union, with
multiple underground militant groups emerging. Soon after, the
AFSPA, which gave the army extraordinary powers, was imposed
in 1980 and a cycle of bloodshed, violence and disturbed peace
has remained ever since.

Caught within the permutations and combinations of these
agendas and conflicts were local civilians, ordinary people with
dreams for their children to not get enmeshed in the violence,
to study and to make a living for themselves. But becoming
enmeshed was inevitable, and it happened during what M
described as the 'dark days of the conflict'.

In November 2003, Lungnila Elizabeth was kidnapped from
outside Little Flower High School in downtown Imphal. A few
days later, her swollen body was found in a swampy area on
the outskirts of Imphal. Lungnila was eight years old, and her
father was Francis Ngajokpa, Manipur's minister for general
administration and taxation.[14]

'She was kidnapped after school was over, and we were all
caught off-guard. We didn't know how to digest it. Kidnappings

are common here, so we all thought she would come back soon. Lungnila was my junior in school; I think a year or two younger than me,' R recollected.

But Lungnila didn't come back.

'All of us found out about her death on the news. The unfiltered description of her dead body, bereft of any sensitivity filter for children, was even more traumatic for me. Her body was bloated because it was dumped in a gunny bag in a swampy area. I still remember those visuals. Her cheeks were swollen. She was still in her uniform,' R conveyed matter-of-factly, while M sat stone-faced as we were having lunch.

But perhaps her work as a lawyer in Manipur also provided her with a 'matter-of-fact' way of narrating these events. 'When we heard the news of her death, the entire school was in mourning. It was a very different situation. No one had faced anything like that. The whole school wept. I have never seen people crying in such large numbers. A few days later, Lungnila's mother came to the school and wept silently. We didn't know how to process all of this; we were all so young. But when we grew up, it was a punch in the gut.'

'Did the school address this?' I asked.

'More than the school, watching TV was adding to the hysteria. The chief minister was crying on TV. The whole grieving process went on for quite some time. We had a prayer session, and condolences came from everywhere, even to us students. The girl's family tried to do a lot for the school in her memory. They built a waiting shed inside the premises, just so that no one would have to wait outside school to get into their transportation. But, yeah, we were back to classes immediately.'

This wasn't the only story I heard about violence in schools or what schools did not do to address trauma, but this indicated to me a hurry, a hurry to move on and not grieve. To grieve was to be consumed by the dehumanization of it all; forgetting seemed to be an easier way.

M and I trudged into the Naga village of Phungyar, located deep inside the hills bordering Myanmar, home to members of the Thangkul tribe. The school that M was helping run was facing staff issues, and M needed to be there to sort it out, and he took me along. On the other side of the hills was Myanmar. Decades of conflict and yearly landslides due to heavy monsoons ensured that very few stretches had motorable roads. 'I never bother washing my car,' M said as we passed through a curtain of dust left behind by the truck in front of us. In a moment, the entire car, its occupants and their luggage were coated in dust. I laughed at what M said as a small cloud of dust descended from my hair. Insurgent groups occasionally blew up roads whose contracts were obtained by rival insurgent groups. The end result was a lack of roads until very recently.

One could deduce that a lack of roads led to a lack of teachers in villages like Phungyar. Moreover, the absence of roads also meant disinterest from government officials, who only very occasionally visited these regions to oversee or inspect any work, especially the functioning of schools. Public schooling was still not a viable option for people in these villages. Public schools existed, but barely so. Most of them were dilapidated, and the ones that managed to survive needed more teachers. 'Teachers don't come here. They make their family their priority. They get recruited by the government after paying a huge bribe, and they don't take their job seriously,' said one of the contracted private teachers at Phungyar High School. Teacher recruitment was a serious problem in India, but especially so in Manipur.

A lack of state apparatus, heavy militarization and lack of roads meant that teachers couldn't be held accountable. M told me that many public schoolteachers took their salaries and never bothered turning up. In fact, some of them had even migrated to some other state and were still receiving their salaries from the government. In their place, some of the public schoolteachers hired private teachers. They were either contracted by the school or the public schoolteachers themselves and were paid a small percentage of the actual salary. In an area where there was hardly any development, paying a few thousand rupees a month to go to private school was a very difficult proposition, yet it remained the only alternative for students who wanted to study their way out of this mess.

Mrs P sat quietly, fiddling with her bag inside the high school in Phungyar. She was a middle-aged woman, her eyes sunken as if weighed down by the depth of whatever she had seen. She seemed reluctant to talk. Yet, Mrs P had responded to my call for some interviews on her experience of violence in Phungyar. I was pleasantly surprised that she turned up, considering the sensitivity of the topic. I had promised to keep her anonymous, and Mrs P agreed to speak in the presence of the principal of the school. She knew M well. M had worked really hard to improve the quality of teaching in the school, and her children were benefiting from it. In any case, I needed M there, as I did everywhere. She spoke only Thangkul, and M translated it for me. She was a quiet woman, and that day, she appeared to be in a dilemma as if she didn't know what to say. She continued fiddling with her bag, pondering what to say and what to leave out. After what felt like ages, she spoke.

National Socialist Council of Nagaland (NSCN) insurgents stormed her house one day, seeking refuge. They were on the run from the army. 'Of course, they were carrying these big guns,' she said, indicating with her arm the size of the guns. Her children were young, one was twelve and the other seven. She quickly rounded up her children and locked them in a room for the rest of the day. At gunpoint, she was held hostage in her own house. As night fell, the insurgents decided to leave for safer refuge through the back door. 'Just as they left, someone knocked on my front door. It was the army. They knew that the insurgents were hiding here,' she said, her voice shaking. If they had stayed, the insurgents would have been shot. It can only be imagined what would have happened to Mrs P and her children. These stories were apparently routine in these regions. M translated Mrs P's stories dispassionately; these stories were all too familiar to him.

'Have you ever spoken about this incident to your children?' I asked, afraid that whatever I might say would be even more triggering. 'No, we have never spoken about it. They are grown-up now,' came the reply from Mrs P. I sensed that she had wanted to share her story. Perhaps there was comfort in narrating these stories for those willing to listen to them. The day after that incident, Mrs P's children were back to school; it was as if nothing had happened. School seemed just a means to get students sufficiently educated to get a job or a certificate signalling their employability. What about the need for a pedagogy through which the teacher and student could situate themselves historically and critically question the structures of power, so that children could become aware of different modes of being, so that they could be aware that their peers, irrespective of who they were, were also probably feeling something similar? There was no time for that, and maybe that was just my understanding of what was needed. And it became evident that education here, like in many other places, was a process of competing priorities, a tug of war to determine what is best for everyone. But the mono-narrative of studying math, science and language continued, just as it did in any other part of the country. 'For parents, it is about getting out of poverty, of getting out of this place. You can't blame them,' M said.

Dusk falls quickly in Manipur. Twilight lasts only a few minutes here. There is daytime, with the sun shining brightly through the dust, and then there's night. It was like there was a switch to turn the sun on and off, as if someone had decided to put a hood over the sun, saying its time was up. Coming from a part of the country where the sunrises and sunsets were almost entirely predictable, where the afternoon heat would soon recede into a cool evening, with the sky adorned in shades of golden red transforming into shades of purple and then finally into nothingness, the evenings in Manipur were a shock. Night came suddenly, and with that, what people felt and did also changed. It was like there was no time to recollect the day, the sunlight, and it was quickly time to pack up and finish up the sparse evening activities and get ready for the next day. I feel that violence and education were considered in much the same way as dusk. It quickly happens, whatever was happening earlier is quickly forgotten, and we prepare for the next day.

* * *

'You should see the spectacle of the Naga Independence Day,' M said during lunch one day. Lunch in this part of the country was eaten at around 9 a.m. or 10 a.m. and included a full plate of rice and some meat, mostly pork or chicken. It was a heavy affair, much like the conversations around violence. 'There's a full live telecast: a weapons' parade and all that. They also hoist the Naga national flag.' The Nagas had created a separate flag for themselves, a blue flag with a diagonal strip of red, yellow and green. This flag had been a huge bone of contention in the peace talks with the Government of India.[15] The Nagas wanted their own nation and to be governed by their own rules. The Nagas, through the Naga National Council (NNC), had declared independence from the British on 14 August 1947, a fact that they hold as a key component in their negotiations for sovereignty. The NNC organized a successful boycott of the 1952 general elections and set up a parallel government. Jawaharlal Nehru found the idea of Naga independence to be 'absurd'.[16] Despite a series of talks with the government, Nehru responded with a violent military campaign.[17] The Naga territories were still rife with these

stories, of solitary doctors being thrown off hill peaks by the army
to ensure no one had access to healthcare, of army men being
waylaid and ambushed, retaliatory death squads that would round
up villagers and shoot them dead, of forced disappearances and
rapes. 'Near my parents' house in Imphal, there is this small hill.
We used to climb up the hill when we were kids. Throughout my
childhood, we would hear gunshots from the hill. In the morning,
we would find a body wrapped in a sack at the bottom of the
hill,' M said.

The insurgency, or to be more accurate, insurgencies, flared
up and down, sometimes reaching pivotal moments, oftentimes
sitting in stalemates and now on the wane. Reconciliation
and integration seemed to be the discourse now, but the small
incidents of violence between stakeholders, big and small, often
went undocumented. Violence was felt and seen, but for how
long do we remember feelings?

Parallel to the violence was a development effort in these
conflict zones. Over the last seventy years, the governments of
Manipur and India built schools and tried to get students to enrol.
The syllabi of these government schools exposed students to the
central and enduring political traditions of India, not of their
tribes or their region. The syllabi fashioned an identity and moral
sentiment required for their performance as effective Indian
citizens, not as Nagas or Kukis, who could also be Indians. In that
manner, the school became an arm of the state to indoctrinate
students towards becoming more Indian. Everyone I spoke
to explained to me the importance of going to school, of the
opportunities it provided. But no one spoke about what the
school did to their identities, or about the dissonance it caused.
The school, as a site for education, was taken for granted, as
it often is.

Here, anger and anguish depended on who had antagonized
you the most. For some, it was the army. For some, it was the

insurgents, and for others, it was the members of another tribe, or the Meiteis living in the Imphal Valley. Borders didn't make much sense either. For the Nagas, their ancestral land was spread across five different states and two countries, and for the Kukis, it was across three states. One day, they were suddenly told that they belonged to the state of Manipur or Nagaland or Assam, to regions and identities that were ascribed to them. In a land where survival could never be taken for granted, everyone learnt their own methods of coping: for some, it was violence, for some forgiveness, and for others hatred.

I spent a few days in Phungyar, mostly inside the government school, talking to teachers and the very enthusiastic principal. The school was rectangular in shape, and there was a yard in the centre where children ran around and played, and classrooms surrounded it. It was a place for students to be watched, not really for them to be seen. I couldn't help but feel how I felt in the Ima Keithel market—cramped, confined, and continuously observed. Except there were no guns, at least at the moment. I didn't have an agenda in the school, and my pointless loitering around, observing classes and talking to teachers roused many people's curiosity.

'Very few people come from outside. It would be nice if you could talk to them,' one of the teachers there told me. I was uncomfortable. I wondered what I could say in this setting; I had taught hundreds of students before, but to speak here unnerved me. 'Just talking to them would give them some exposure,' the teacher insisted. I was still unsure. I decided I would ask these students questions instead; it would save me the difficulty of saying something.

The class was packed with teenagers, noisy and somewhat rowdy, as most classrooms filled with teenagers are. After getting them to settle down, I asked them what they wanted to do after finishing school, a banal question, but what else could I have asked or said? One boy sheepishly raised his hand. 'I want to join the army,' he said. Immediately, another boy also raised his hand. 'Sir, I also want to join the army.' And like this, power structures continued to reproduce themselves in these lands, in a vicious cycle. 'Why do you want to join the army?' I asked. The students kept silent. Their silence spoke a thousand words.

* * *

Late one night, M and I were sitting in our room at a dingy lodge in the village of Phungyar. All the shops had closed. In Nagaland and Manipur, the day ends by 4.30 p.m. or 5 p.m., with the sudden blackening of the sky. For decades, legislators, activists, scholars, industrialists and citizens have asked for a different time zone for the Northeast. The difference between the easternmost point in India to the westernmost is over 2500 km. Keeping a uniform time zone over such large distances meant that in the summer Nagaland and Manipur would see sunrise as early as 5 a.m. and in the winters, the sun set as early as 3.30 p.m. Bangladesh, which shares land borders with Assam, Meghalaya, Tripura and Mizoram is in a different time zone, 30 minutes ahead of the Indian Standard Time (IST). The CSIR-National Physical Laboratory (CSIR-NPL) and the National Measurement Institute (NMI) of India have proposed the implementation of two time zones for the country,[18] only for it to be customarily ignored, as it has been for decades now. People usually eat their dinners by 6 p.m. and are tucked in bed by 8 p.m. In any case, being out on the roads late at night is dangerous. Army patrols can pick you up under suspicion. My body slowly started adjusting to this new routine; I was not all used to being in bed by 8 p.m. Normally, it is when my night starts. But the silence of the night has its own weight; it creeps on you and then drags you slowly towards slumber. A week or so into my time in Manipur, I was falling fast asleep by 9 p.m., something I have not been able to replicate ever since.

M never once asked me why I was asking him these questions, why I wanted to write this book or what I wanted to do on this trip. He simply took me along with him everywhere, and even after I left Manipur, responded quickly to my calls for clarification. I often wondered why, and I wondered what I would tell him if he ever did ask. But he never did.

'We are going to Kamjong tomorrow,' said M excitedly, even as we both tiredly yawned around 7.30 p.m. after a day of working at the school. Kamjong was where M and his brothers were born and raised. He traced his Kamjong ancestors back to hundreds of years. It was a Naga-dominated area, and M spoke Thangkul, also the name of the tribe he belonged to. M also spoke six other dialects. Each village in the Naga hills had its own language, many of them mutually unintelligible.

Kamjong was a hill district, and being a hill district, it had a low population density. The problems of the hill people weren't just limited to the excesses of the army, the continuous terror of insurgents or even to inter-tribal conflict. Political representation was a burning issue as well. The Manipur legislative seat had sixty-six seats. Out of these seats, forty were for representatives within the Imphal Valley and twenty-six for the rest of the hills.[19]

'Kamjong is a district, it is almost 2000 square kilometres in size. It is bigger than Imphal city, but we only have one MLA,' M said, angrily looking out of the window. Not a soul moved outside. The air was still. 'When the Meiteis have forty seats, they obviously control everything. The chief minister will obviously not be a Naga. How is this fair political representation?'

While political representation was fraught with dilemmas, another method to balance power between the Meiteis, Nagas and Kukis was conceived by the Indian government. Affirmative action had given greater chances to the Nagas within the Indian bureaucratic structure.

'Reservation has helped us, though. All of us Nagas have a scheduled tribe status,' said M. 'A lot of the bureaucrats in the

Manipur government are Nagas or Kukis. So, now, the Meiteis feel alienated. They are not able to get government jobs that easily.'

The Meiteis had been demanding scheduled tribe status too, something that the Nagas had vociferously been protesting against. In the 2023 conflict between the Meiteis and Kukis in Manipur, which dominated headlines in mainland India for several months, this issue again flared up with the Meitei clamour for a scheduled tribe status increasing.

Bandhs (general strikes) and blockades were common in Manipur. When there was a bandh, all shops would be closed, and no vehicles would be allowed to ply on the road in Imphal. In the hills, the situation was the same. It was just another aspect of life, similar to the continued military presence. 'You can't get anything done; you just have to sit at home,' M said.

For someone new to this part of the world, every Sunday would feel like a bandh in itself. While the Meiteis in the Imphal Valley were predominantly Hindu, the tribes in the hills were almost all Christians. Every Sunday, people dressed in their finest and went to church. Nothing would be open, no shops and no means of transport. Entire settlements would resemble ghost towns. It just so happened that I was in these hills during two separate bandhs. The still nights and the bandhs were all exercises in emptiness. The bandh days were long and dreary, and I often considered writing during those days, but the emptiness weighed on my motivation. Within an emptiness, another one grew, and I realized that this is a hallmark of that theme, its unending ability to open up more abysses.

* * *

The drive up to Kamjong was surprisingly smooth. The roads had just been laid and black-topped. M's car chugged along smoothly on these fresh velvet-like roads. M had bought a four-wheeled drive, a Maruti Gypsy, from an army auction a few years ago at a throwaway price, and the car could navigate through feet of slush, which often happened when it rained. But slush resulted from a lack of roads, and now there were roads.

Throughout the journey, we talked excitedly about crossing the border and going to Myanmar. Kamjong shares a long international porous border with Myanmar, and from Kamjong, smaller towns of the Myanmar border are easily accessible. But the COVID-19 pandemic dealt a harsh blow to our plans. The border had increased security now.

M pulled up at the army check-post outside Kamjong. Every vehicle passing by had to stop, so that the occupants could enter their names into a log and subject themselves to checking. M got out of the car and went inside the outpost, to fill in the details of the car and give my details as well. Meanwhile, a burly army officer, gun in hand, came towards the car. He peered into the front and looked into my eyes for a few seconds. He moved to the back and looked at the two women sitting at the back, M's colleagues and friends. My body was tense and I looked straight ahead. Seemingly satisfied, the army officer beckoned that we were good to go. M got into the car and drove straight ahead. None of us made eye contact with the army personnel.

The uniforms, the guns, the stares, the armed vehicles—if ever there was an omnipresent being in Manipur, it was the armed men in uniforms, a constant reminder that the people of Manipur were Indian, or rather, they had to be. The fear amongst people in Manipur was omnipresent, except it didn't have any god-like values. I asked M about this feeling of fear and whether it permeates in schools as well. 'It's everywhere, especially in schools,' laughed S from the back of the car.

S was always ready to talk. She was a teacher working in a government school, as part of M's organization. S was energetic, with a bounce in their gait, as if she were fuelled by energy drinks all day. All one had to do was allow her to talk, a pleasure for someone like me struggling to ask the next question in such a conflicted region. She had grown up in insurgency-hit Manipur and had decided to be a teacher, for she believed she could teach her way out of this mess.

If homes, like the house of Mrs P, weren't a safe refuge for insurgents, schools were. The campuses of far-flung, dilapidated public schools in these small villages provided excellent cover for insurgents on the run from the army. The hills were rife with stories of school walls riddled with bullet holes and smeared with bloodstains left by the army, insurgents and even local neighbours. The conflicts were multipolar and complex, and it was reductive to blame just one violent perpetrator. Often, students and teachers were complicit in aiding and abetting this violence inside the schools. In conflict zones, schools seemed to have multiple purposes. They not only provided people with hope for a better future but also offered refuge to people on the run.

S and two other girls lived on the campus of one such school. 'Once our programme manager came to visit us; it was just a group of four girls in our room inside the school. Usually, after a day at school, we wind down and just chill,' continued A. 'It was 7.30 p.m., and we were settling in. Someone knocked on the door.'

'Was it usual for someone to knock on your door at that time?' I asked.

'Not really, but we weren't too worried. We were too lazy to get up, so we just shouted to whoever was outside to come in.'

The door burst open, and a group of army men, rifles loaded, stood at the entrance. 'They came in and started asking all sorts of questions—who we are, why are we here, where are we from . . .' The soldiers searched every room and checked every nook and cranny as the women stood there, powerless and fearful. Since it was clear that the girls weren't hiding anyone, the soldiers left. But it was yet another incident that proved nothing could be taken for granted, especially the sanctity of a school. A site of education had become a site of violence.

For people like S, it was not just the insurgents that were the antagonists, but it was the army as well.

Simultaneously, the fear was also scattered and diffusive; it circulated amongst different people in different contexts. Ultimately, it produced differentiation between 'us' and 'them', that is, fear created boundaries and informed every interaction.

If there was a conflict of identity here, the inherent sense of identity and pride amongst the different tribes in Manipur added more layers to it.

It was late one night when members of the Kuki tribe in the village of Chasad, next to Kamjong, found their jhum cultivation burned to ashes. The perpetrators of the crime were never identified, but it was alleged that it was the Thangkul Nagas from the neighbouring village.[20] The Kukis and Nagas had a long history of ethnic clashes, mostly over land disputes.

The necessity of guarding one's village against invaders and foes has long been intrinsic to Nagas' political history.[21] 'Nagas always want to keep some land in the village, even if they hardly come there. Without land, it is difficult to claim that you belong to a village, and without belonging to a village, it is difficult to claim you are a Naga,' explained the village headman of Kasom Khulem, another village in the district of Kamjong. I had gone to Kasom Khulem, not too far from Phungyar or Kamjong, for a meeting with the Naga village council, facilitated by M, to get a grasp on the importance of land for identity.

In these regions, Naga–Kuki relations were tense at best. The peak of the conflict was in the 1990s. Families hid in underground shelters, even in winter, while armed men roamed the streets looking to kill members of the other tribe. Adult male members were armed and tasked with guarding the village.[22] The 1990s saw enormous violence and death amongst the Nagas and the Kukis, but life still went on, with land conflicts remaining the dominant narrative.

'No one took any action. Everyone was indifferent towards it,' M said as we continued driving up. This indifference and lack of action enraged the Kukis. In March 2020, they declared a blockade, not allowing any vehicles to pass through. They also set fire to a Naga-owned petrol pump in Kamjong.

'I was there when this happened. I called the village committee and told them not to do anything further for this would only escalate,' M said. But his words fell on deaf ears. The Nagas decided to 'finish them off'.

The next morning, groups of men armed with stones, logs, knives and spears descended on Chasad.

M drove past a part of the village of Chasad. There it stood. What once was a settlement with hundreds of houses had now been replaced with blackened stumps of trees all around, with the construction of tin houses in progress. The entire village was being reconstructed, tin sheet by tin sheet, by the government, on top of burnt remains. Like elsewhere, the implicit message here was to forget and move on. What else could one do?

The entire village had been burned down; over 200 houses were reduced to ashes. The inhabitants had fled into nearby jungles. Hiding there, they watched their homes, utensils, savings, documents and memories burn.

'The army did nothing. They were right there. They saw what was happening and could have come in to stop the entire thing,' M continued as we entered Kamjong.

This incident was still bothering him. To have witnessed the burning down of an entire village was certain to have left anyone traumatized.

Kamjong was a small town. There were definitely more shops than in Phungyar or Kasom Khulem, but the town had an ironical aura of serenity. Anthropologist Kimberly Theidon in her work on facing the past in post-conflict zones writes, 'Co-existence is based on a complete alchemy of remembering, forgetting and remembering to forget'.[23] This seemed to apply in Kamjong.

The public school at Kamjong was on a flattened part of the hill. A large tract of land served as a football ground, while the school buildings lay right behind it, arranged in a rectangular pattern. Potted plants adorned the corridors, giving the entire school and classrooms a feel of serenity, a setting quite the opposite of what happened outside its campus. Perhaps, the school was a refuge, an escape from the pervasive tension, but, in its presence and functioning, it could only mask the tension and never fully hide it.

'I came to the school soon after this incident had happened. This is the only school in the area. Kuki as well as Naga students come here to study. There were a lot of students from Chasad here,' said one of the teachers. 'I can still see shadows of the incident continuously lurking.'

Then, she told me what happened. Even though most students were peaceful and amicable to their classmates, there were one or two older children who incited hateful thoughts in the minds of other children. 'After school was over, all the older Naga kids were waiting for Kuki students just outside the school. They were threatening them and calling them to a particular location for a chat. Obviously, there was not going to be a chat. The other kids knew what was going to happen.'

The school had become a site of violence in itself. 'We had to call the student union, which is powerful here, and even the village headman to ensure the safety of our students,' the teacher continued. 'After school, we also had to drop children back to Chasad every day. The kids would point to the burned sites of their homes and fields and share their memories with us.'

Detailed research in trauma education has shown that in trauma-oriented groups, the individual's identity becomes more strongly linked to his or her group identity and enemy perception. Moreover, the prevalent conception of the 'other' as a fixed category, that is, the enemy, dangerously increases the tendency to dehumanize the other.[24] The category of 'the other' subsumed existing friendships among students in Kamjong, leading them to forget that 'the other' was a category that consisted of human beings. It was perhaps inevitable. Despite the school's best efforts, the trauma of seeing your own house being burnt by your friend's family members only served to increase the feeling of fear and hatred.

Soon, the effort and burden of having to walk the children back to their village proved too much for the teachers. The students had to walk through long areas of Naga territory, a proposition that made everyone uncomfortable. In a few months, all the Kuki students had stopped coming, and their education halted. The families in Chasad all decided that they would set up their own tuitions and coaching, pulling their children out of school.

'As teachers, we couldn't tell them to come back and promise that everything would be fine. We could guarantee their safety inside the campus, but when they left, they would still have to walk through Kamjong. They didn't feel safe in doing so,' said the teacher at the school.

Just as in the Phungyar school, tension was never discussed in this school, through the curriculum or even through conversations. No one particularly questioned even if it should have been brought up. Routinized classes of math and science draped a veil over the tension and trauma that the students faced outside. Perhaps because the teachers themselves never completely reconciled with their tension or trauma.

The student was taught his or her mother tongue—Thangkul to the Nagas and Thadouw to the Kukis. Identities were being reinforced in school, and sometimes new identities were created. The identity began at home, but the school was a site for its reaffirmation, for better or for worse.

'Christmas is a very important festival in the hills,' M said while we drank cups of very sweet tea on one of the last days of my time in Manipur. 'Christianity came to the hill tribes through American, British and Welsh missionaries in the early 1900s, and almost everyone adopted it. But this conversion also required us to let go of particular rituals and tasks intimate to our identity. For my forefathers, it was almost a new lifestyle. Christmas is when everyone celebrates here, irrespective of any differences they have.'

'Do you guys exchange a lot of gifts?' I asked.

'Yes, of course. A lot. But the only thing kids want for Christmas these days is guns,' M sighed as the afternoon suddenly turned to night, as it usually did.

Entire generations had grown up closely involved with violence. They had had family members tortured, dismembered and killed. They had seen villages burn and had gone for days without essential supplies. The idea of education has always given people hope—to study was to imagine new possibilities and perhaps a more peaceful future. But without scope for empathy and reconciliation of trauma, education seemed to only provide the illusion of hope.

The narratives of fear, violence and anger were also sites of education, for they consumed everyone and subsumed everything. One of the purposes of a school is to build peace, but when tension and trauma aren't integrated within the education being delivered, schools also become sites of violence. In that, the promise of education—of being a harbinger of peace, of being a promoter of economic opportunities—and an opportunity to 'assimilate' remains unrealized. But in such a conflict zone, the promise of education itself seemed poorly conceived and conceived in a hurry. Moreover, education was being administered under the pretext of the nation, to make children better citizens. No one asked or cared what really mattered. In these hills and this valley, seeing and feeling violence constituted education.

Chapter 3

Tap That Toddy

'For me, a theory of justice cannot, and should not, provide a comprehensive account of the overall goodness or badness of society. Rather, it should allow us to evaluate social arrangements from the perspective of one limited, but extremely important angle: how fair or unfair are the terms of interaction that are institutionalized in the society?'

—Nancy Fraser[1]

I had no idea where Vembar was or how to get there. I just knew that I had to, because a man called Rajesh, whom I had only spoken to on the phone once, had promised to take me around the palmyra tree plantations in that place and tell me everything he could about it. 'Palmyra trees are our education, Sir,' he said.

Shortly after the COVID-19 pandemic hit in full swing in India, I was on the ground in southern and western Tamil Nadu, travelling with senior politicians of the DMK on the campaign trail for the 2021 Tamil Nadu Legislative Assembly elections, helping design and organize their rallies and campaigns. Pandemic or not, the election juggernaut had to keep rolling.

In January 2021, as lockdown restrictions eased, huge crowds thronged rallies. In many of the rallies I attended, the crowd appeared rather impatient and their mood indignant. While the politicians were on stage, I would walk through the crowds asking anyone I could about what they felt about the upcoming elections and what issues they wanted to address. More often than not, education and employment came up. '*Vellaiye ille*, Sir; there are no jobs at all' was something I kept hearing. One such rally was organized for a group of palmyra tree climbers in the rural constituency of Omalur, located in the district of Salem in western Tamil Nadu. The crowd was furious. They felt that multiple governments had not listened to their grievances about the dire state of the profession, about the discrimination they faced and about the bleak futures they and their children were looking at. It was in this context that the idea for this story and, in many ways, the contours of this book emerged as well. Climbing palmyra trees, collecting the sap, making palm sugar and brewing a potent and delicious liquor called toddy (*kallu* in Tamil) was an indigenous profession that has been documented in Tamil literature for at least a thousand years. How was globalization affecting the futures of these climbers and their children and how were modern educational systems shaping it? How were palmyra trees their education, as Rajesh had mentioned?

Vembar was a dot on the map of Tamil Nadu. The plethora of places, their names, their landscapes, and their people often remain only a data point, an indication that they exist, an affirmation that we are all part of one large world that we can make sense of. The oneness of the world, a globalized view—a dream for many and a serious project for a powerful few—perhaps only exists in our imaginations, sometimes blurred, often invisible.

The little village of Vembar was in the midst of the politics of globalization, and education had played a huge part in its current situation.

To get to Vembar, I knew I had to go to the Thoothukudi railway station, an overnight train journey from Chennai. From the Thoothukudi railway station, I had to get to the bus terminus, catch a bus to Ramanathapuram and get off on the way at Vembar, a coastal village on the border of the districts of Thoothukudi and Ramanathapuram in Tamil Nadu. If one faced north, to one's right, one could see the vast Bay of Bengal and its waves caressing the shore, bordered by acres and acres of salt pans. To one's left, slightly away from the never-ending ocean, hundreds of palmyra trees jutted out of the ground—most of them straight as a pencil, some crooked and twisted and a solitary one that resembled the spine of a person with bad posture. The palmyra tree is a symbol of life to the people in this region. It gives them everything—a source of livelihood and an identity; it figures in their politics, and as I later found out, it also had a serious effect on their education.

I met Rajesh at the bus stop in Vembar, a small structure decked in the banners of various political parties. Just next to it, there were two small eateries, selling idlis, dosas and puris, and a small store. Rajesh had come on his bike, with an extra helmet ready. He was a small man, but well-built, and his face exuded a look of determination and resolve. I must have looked tired and haggard. I could sense him looking at me and sizing me up. Who was this guy who had come to talk to him about palmyra trees? 'Lots to see, sir,' he said, as I got on his bike, even as I longed for some coffee. But we had to see palmyra trees and talk about them first.

Many people in Vembar and its surrounding areas are associated with the palmyra trees. A lot of them come from families who climb the palmyra tree to harvest its products. Many retail the products obtained, and almost all are affected by the economics and the politics surrounding the trees. In a region where the soil and groundwater are too saline for agriculture, the palmyra tree has more than made up for it. It produces delicious fruit (*nongu*). Its sap (*padhineer*) is used to make palm jaggery and palm sugar, and its dried leaves can be used as roofing or to thatch baskets. 'A single tree can give you 20 to 25 kilograms of jaggery, around 10 kilograms of leaves, and 20 kilograms of palm fibre. Plus, we can also make 15 to 20 kilograms of palm candy. All from a single tree,' said Kamaraj with pride. Rajesh had randomly stopped his bike in the middle of a narrow highway a little outside Vembar and introduced me to Kamaraj just as he was about to climb a tree. At sixty, Kamaraj looked fitter than an athlete in his prime, though the shades of grey in his hair and beard gave him the look of an embattled soldier. His shoulders and back were toned and muscular, and he sported a set of abs that would make a Bollywood actor insecure. Kamaraj was a palmyra tree climber, and he had been one for forty-seven years.

'We start our day at 2.30 a.m. We have to climb the tree and make an incision in the inflorescence and set up pots to collect the sap. Only if we climb by 2.30 a.m. can we bring down the padhineer by 7 a.m. After some breakfast, I climb again at 9 a.m. and continue the same process of setting up pots to collect the padhineer. Then, I climb again at 3.30 p.m. to bring down all the pots filled with padhineer. We repeat this process every day for six months,' Kamaraj explained.

Climbing palmyra trees has traditionally been a male-dominated profession. The men climb the trees and bring down the padhineer, while the women boil it to make *karupatti*, the delicious palm jaggery and the main source of income for palmyra tree climbers in the state today.

'Some trees give 200 millilitres of padhineer, some 500 millilitres, and some even give 2 litres. On an average, we can get 2 to 3 litres per tree per day,' Kamaraj said as he fastened his foot harness. In a minute, he was at the top of a 40-foot-tall, pencil-straight tree, replacing a pot filled with padhineer with an empty one. The foot harness was just a piece of cloth that bound his feet together. Holding the trunk of the tree with his palms and clasping his feet around the tree, in a few swift motions, he had scaled it.

The season to collect padhineer is only four to six months long, starting from mid-February or early March and continuing up until August. The palmyra tree diffuses sap only during these months, so utilizing every day of this season is imperative. 'On an average, I used to be able to climb forty-five trees a day. But I have become old now. I climb only twenty-five trees a day. I get joint pains in my knees. My wrists hurt. Once you grow old, you don't have the *surusuruppu*.' (*Surusuruppu* is Tamil for energy and enthusiasm.)

The padhineer collected from the palmyra tree is useful and controversial. The boiling of the padhineer produces karupatti, which is as sweet as refined sugar but without its health risks. From the karupatti, one can make palm sugar. The pots in which the padhineer is collected is coated with *sunaambu* (slaked lime) to avoid fermentation. This bit is straightforward. But if the padhineer were allowed to ferment, it would yield toddy, a mildly alcoholic beverage banned in Tamil Nadu since 1987 and the source of all controversy and politics for palmyra tree climbers across the state. Ever since the ban on toddy in Tamil Nadu by the M.G. Ramachandran-led AIADMK government many years ago, palmyra tree climbers have had no choice but to use padhineer only for making karupatti.

Income levels in the region are not exactly high. Land owning isn't much of a concept either, for much of the land in the region is affected by salinity. People who didn't own land would do what Anthony Chevaram did. He took loans of a few lakh rupees and rented out an acre of land that had anywhere between 200 to 400 trees. 'Beyond the rent and living expenses, we are able to make 2 to 3 lakhs a year selling karupatti,' said Anthony. But that was never enough, for the interest rates of the loans were exorbitantly high, up to 24 to 30 per cent a year, and paying back the loans ate into all the profits the tree climbers made. Anthony was a palmyra tree climber and lived in a temporary hut made of palm fronds in the middle of a large patch of land full of palmyra trees on both sides. He was a tall, well-built man with a round face that made him look a lot younger than he actually was. His arms and feet were dry and cracking from the continuous abrasion of his skin against the rough bark of the tree.

The palmyra tree climbers and their families worked hard through the padhineer-collecting season; as soon as the padhineer was brought down, the women would start the boiling process to make karupatti. This process wasn't an easy one either since the women had to light wood-fired stoves and continuously stir the liquid, all while keeping a careful eye on it and inhaling all the smoke.

Vembar was a coastal village, and the soil was saline, affecting the growth of the trees and the padhineer. A short distance away lay the village of Sayalgudi, where the soil was clayey and could retain more water. Here, the trees reportedly didn't just give sweeter padhineer but also yielded higher quantities. It was here that Anthony had rented out land. He wasn't allowed to build a permanent shelter on the rented land and so a hut from palm fronds had to do. The cooking was done outdoors. Once a week, Anthony's son would bring water in a big drum for cooking and drinking.

* * *

Once the karupatti was made, it would be given to a *vyabari* (Tamil for trader), but in this profession, really a middleman. Middlemen have long been considered essential in business, for they help the manufacturer reach the consumer. But in the case of the karupatti in Vembar, a lack of access to markets had left palmyra tree climbers like Anthony and Kamaraj at the mercy of these exploitative middlemen.

'We don't get loans from banks. They don't even entertain us. We rely on these vyabaris, whom we pay to get loans. They charge exorbitant interest rates, but what choice do we have?' sighed

Yesthov, on the highway between Vembar and Sayalgudi. He had just climbed down from a tree with an armful of the delicious palmyra fruit, nongu.

Yesthov pointed to the other side of the highway, to a man on top of a palmyra tree. 'That man owes Rs 4 lakh to a vyabari. He also sells his karuppati to the same vyabari. But what happens is that just before he is going to sell his entire stock, the vyabari changes the price of the karupatti. All these moneylenders gang up and change prices, so there's nothing anyone can do about it. They reduce prices suddenly towards the end of the season and then sell at high rates in outside markets, by saying it's the end of the season. I sell my karupatti to the vyabari only. Who else can I sell it to? Including interest, I have a loan of Rs 3 lakh now. I have to work the entire year to pay the money back,' sighed Yesthov. All the profits and the money that the climbers were making were going into repaying loans, whose interest kept compounding every year.

Kotpandi Raju, his wife and his grandchildren were sitting inside their temporary hut. The leaves of the palmyra tree were never large enough to give shade, and in the southern regions of Tamil Nadu, the sun beamed upon the land with a vengeance. Kotpandi Raju claimed he was sixty but looked older. His body exhibited the remnants of a once-toned musculature, and he looked burdened. But, when the question of the vyabaris came up, his expression immediately changed to indignation. 'These vyabaris form syndicates and control the price of karupatti. The going rate for karupatti is actually Rs 2800 to 3000 for 10 kilograms. But they give us only Rs 1500 to 1600. The problem is that we climbers can only put *jalra* to the vyabaris (suck up to the middlemen) because they control the loans. They will only give loans to the people they like. They eat our profits!' The climbers mentioned that they had to remain in the good books of these vyabaris for they didn't just control the rate of interest, but they also controlled the rate of the karupatti.

Temporary settlements were few and far between in vast tracts of land that had only palmyra trees shooting out of the ground, and the people who had taken up these lands for rent lived lives of relative isolation during the season when they climbed the trees. Between September and February, most of them moved back to their homes within the village of Vembar and rested, allowing their bodies to recover. But that wasn't an option all could exercise. The income from climbing for six months was never completely sufficient to pay back loans. Some went out to sea to fish; some moved to bigger towns in search of work.

At first sight, Vembar was serene and idyllic. The palmyra leaves swayed ever so slightly, and the land was flat. But like in many other serene and idyllic settings, it held many problems deep in its belly.

* * *

In August 2020, the Madras High Court directed the state government of Tamil Nadu to undertake an extensive process of enumerating and enlisting all unorganized workers in the state under thirty-four different welfare boards constituted for their benefit.[2] At the time of writing, palmyra tree climbers were not enlisted under any of the welfare boards present in the state. The welfare boards constituted a threat to the existence of the middlemen. These boards had the capacity to issue licenses, regulate prices and collectively protect the climbers from exploitation. Additional benefits of being part of a welfare board included scholarships, insurance, training and even funeral assistance. But the palmyra tree climbers in Vembar could not access any of this.

'There is an association of palmyra tree climbers here, but it is of absolutely no use. We earlier got a licence card through them, but what is the point of that? No one recognizes it, and there is no benefit for us in it,' said Devasagayam, another palmyra tree climber, while cutting open some ripe nongu to eat, on the outskirts of Vembar. The tone in his voice suggested that the climbers had given up on any hope of institutional support. What use was a tool of identification if no one recognized it?

Kotpandi Raju elaborated further on the issue. 'We first had a palmyra tree climbers' *sangam* (society). But the vyabaris came in and said if we have a sangam, they would refuse to give us loans. We don't even have a card from the palmyra tree climbers' sangam. These vyabaris won't even let us get a sangam card, because we can use that card and get a loan somewhere else. Ask anyone in this region if they have a card. They won't! There was a sangam inside Padineer Mahal in VVR Nagar (a short distance away from Sayalgudi). But the vyabaris burnt it down.' This was an informal association; the climbers had made multiple attempts to organize themselves and get collective recognition, only for it to be thwarted every time. Successive governments had also paid no heed to their requests to set up a formal welfare board.

In Vembar and Sayalgudi, it was as if the vyabaris had collectively denied any form of recognition or redistribution to the climbers. The climbers seemed to have lost all hope of any form of formal recognition, either through the government or through their own process of organizing themselves. From their tone of conversation, it was evident that they had reconciled to just work hard and fend for themselves.

Like most other climbers, Devasagayam, Yesthov and Kotpandi Raju all belonged to the Nadar caste. Traditionally, the caste was engaged in its hereditary occupation as toddy tappers and climbers of the palmyra. Defiled by their ritually impure calling, they suffered the social disabilities of a low, almost untouchable, community. At the beginning of the nineteenth century, the Nadars or the Shanars, as they were then known, were almost entirely engaged in the cultivation and climbing of the palmyra.[3] In time, they began migrating to other Tamil Nadu cities, such as Madurai, where they settled as traders and merchants and acquired a degree of status and power. But the contradiction between their traditionally low social status and their rising economic status continued to rankle. Seeking the upliftment of the entire community and to attempt to move ahead in the caste hierarchy, the Nadar traders organized the Nadar Mahajana Sangam in 1910.[4] This caste association soon became the largest and most active in all of Tamil Nadu. They established a cooperative bank, and schools and colleges were founded, with scholarships being given to Nadar students. However, not all reaped the benefits; many continued the profession of climbing palmyra trees.[5]

What could change the fortunes of those left behind? The legalization of toddy was a matter burdened by history. The reason for the ban on toddy is a result of the convoluted story of prohibition in the state and its reversal over the past many decades.

From 1948 to 1971, the production and consumption of liquor was banned across the state. Support for prohibition at that time cut across party lines. In 1971, M. Karunanidhi of the DMK ended the prohibition on arrack, toddy and Indian-Made Foreign Liquor (IMFL). Karunanidhi's rationale for lifting the ban was that unless prohibition was imposed across India, other states that permitted liquor would continue to profit from it. Tamil Nadu, meanwhile, was missing out. In 1974, it imposed prohibition, yet again, firstly of arrack and then of IMFL, hoping to reap political benefits. As liquor consumption went underground, bootlegging spiked, leading to two incidents in 1975 and 1976 when many died due to the consumption of spurious liquor. M.G. Ramachandran of the All-India Anna Dravida Munnetra Kazhagam won the state elections in 1977 and was chief minister for three consecutive terms. Though Ramachandran had called strongly for prohibition while not in power, he lifted the ban on arrack and toddy in his second term in 1981, this time under heavy state monitoring and five separate laws.[6]

From 1982 to 1983, the government allowed the private sector to begin manufacturing IMFL in Tamil Nadu. Then in 1983 came the Tamil Nadu State Marketing Corporation (TASMAC), which monopolized the wholesale trade of arrack and Indian-made foreign spirits. In 1991, the AIADMK, this time under J. Jayalalithaa, banned arrack and toddy. This ban on the manufacture and sale of country liquor lasted for more than a decade.

In November 2003, TASMAC took over the entire retail liquor business. Alcohol was actively promoted by district collectors through fixed sales targets. The stated objective was 'to completely eliminate the sale of contraband, spurious liquor that affects the health of the liquor consuming public'.[7] In 2023, revenue from TASMAC was close to Rs 44,000 crore, a quarter of the entire revenue of the state.[8]

For a long time, tree climbers like Rajesh and others had dealt with exploitative vyabaris, casteist slurs and difficulty in making money. Sustained welfare politics from successive Dravidian governments gave them a peek into a world of development and aspirations. They didn't want to be left behind like their forefathers. Within the realm of climbing palmyra trees, boiling karupatti and tapping toddy, they wanted to be recognized for who they were: Nadars, whose families had climbed palmyra trees and tapped toddy for generations.

For days, Rajesh took me around on his bike to meet palmyra tree climbers while giving me colourful and elaborate commentary on the Tamil Nadu government's monopoly on alcohol distribution. The notion of education hung like an umbrella over our conversations; he spoke vividly about how some in Vembar had studied engineering and seemed to be in dignified spaces and rued how palmyra tree climbers continued to be treated with contempt. 'Palmyra tree climbing has been mentioned in Tamil literature for 2000 years, and now, suddenly, it is undesirable. Why is studying engineering considered okay but not studying climbing palmyra trees? Do you know there is a college in Kerala that teaches coconut tree climbing?' he sighed as we rode through the continuously shifting landscapes of palmyra trees, salt pans and beaches. Here, like in many other professions, the politics of dignity and poverty worked hand in hand. But Rajesh had already built a sense of dignity around himself, and with it came aspirations, a desire to aspire towards a better future and not meekly accept his fate.

'There is a saying in our village: *Kallu arunthavan, Karuthai elunthavan. Mathu arunthavan, Madhiyai elunthavan* (The man who drinks toddy temporarily loses his opinion; the man who drinks alcohol loses his mind). Do you know what the government and people are saying? They're saying don't tap toddy because it is harmful for life. They are saying that we bring it down at 6 a.m. and get people drunk in the morning. Only in Tamil Nadu, it is banned. You get toddy in Kerala and Karnataka,' continued Rajesh angrily, standing under the hot sun as we sipped some unfermented padhineer.

'That is all okay, but out of hundred, if only ten people keep shouting, no one is going to listen,' interjected Rajesh's friend.

Rajesh continuously referred to government-run alcohol shops (TASMAC) as 'Satan's den' and the alcohol sold in them as 'Satan's piss'. The anger was evident, and I often sat quietly listening to his tirade. In his passionate narrative, Rajesh often forgot time as well. We would stand under some palmyra tree somewhere outside Vembar, and he would elaborate on his rant, while the people we were to meet would be waiting.

The palmyra tree climbers now aspired for something that they believed would be a game changer—the legitimacy of state intervention with toddy being given recognition by the state, in the same way that IMFL had gained legitimacy of sorts after being labelled as '*Arasanga Sarayam*' (government liquor). The unrest about the ban on toddy found resonance among palmyra tree climbers in Vembar and Sayalgudi. The legalization of toddy would allow for the value of the tree to be unlocked and the incomes of the palmyra tree climbers to increase exponentially. The government could legalize and levy tax on the sale of toddy and augment its revenues as well, making it a win-win for all. But these demands have fallen on deaf ears. Moral arguments against the brewing of home-made and illicit liquor have prevented politicians from actively taking up and representing these causes. The hope that the climbers had pinned on the state welfare boards has long since vanished, with the climbers turning their demands directly to the government.

In terms of remuneration, despite the difficulties posed by the vyabaris and the demanding nature of this profession, a palmyra tree climber could rake in anywhere between Rs 2 to 10 lakh a year in profit. This is, of course, without the burden of any loans that beleaguered almost every climber I met. Arguably, this was more than what an entry-level engineer or a private schoolteacher could make in a city in Tamil Nadu, and yet as Rajesh, Antony and others had remarked more than once, their children did not want to be part of the tree-climbing profession. Clearly, it was not the money that was driving the children of these climbers out of these professions. It had to do with the indignity of it. Public education had provided the community with a window into a seemingly more dignified world, into a global economy. Education dangled the hope of formal employment—a white-collared world that offered greater dignity, despite lower pay.

But would education guarantee employment? The spectre of unemployment or underemployment also hung in the air. This is not to argue against education but to make the point that education in Tamil Nadu had to be looked at in conjunction with several other social forces in play.

Education had certainly played a role in opening up certain opportunities and had served as a means to undermine established structures of power, to enable social and economic mobility for some Nadars. But at the same time, it drew palm-tree climbers even more tightly into narratives and structures of dominance, where they had to look for secure, 'status-saving' jobs. If they didn't get the desired 'status-saving' employment, caste-based discrimination and biases would continue and reproduce in newer forms, and they would be condemned to low-paying, precarious jobs.[9]

* * *

Palmyra trees grow in different parts of the state and large plantations of palmyra trees can be found all over. Mukkudal, a village in Tirunelveli district, was another site where palmyra trees were aplenty. Unlike Vembar, where the soil was affected by salinity, Mukkudal was far away from the coast, and agriculture thrived along with palmyra plantations.

Mukkudal was a small, self-contained village. Life around the village revolved around palmyra trees and the church in the village centre. All of them were Nadar Christians. Rajesh had connected me to his friend Arul Yenbaraj in Mukkudal. Arul was a seller of palmyra tree produce; he was not a tree climber but bought the produce from his kin and sold it in the town of Tirunelveli, where people bought a lot of palm sugar as a replacement for refined sugar. Arul took me along on his bike and explained the commonalities and the differences between the tree-climbing profession of Mukkudal and Vembar.

Like Vembar's, most of Mukkudal's climbers were Nadars. But unlike Vembar and Sayalgudi, the palmyra tree climbers of Mukkudal had a union (sangam) and also an identity card confirming their membership. Membership in this sangam allowed them to get a pension and obtain a minimum monthly salary. What was left of the corpus was split evenly among the members. The profit primarily went to the climbers. Vyabaris didn't exist any more in Mukkudal. The produce was sold either through the sangam or people bought directly from the climbers. It struck me that the frustration that Kotpandi Raju and the others had in Vembar didn't completely reflect here. But there were commonalities too.

The ban on toddy irked the people in Mukkudal as well. 'It will be great if they get rid of this ban. But, of course, the government won't. Who will go to TASMAC then? One quarter (of liquor) costs Rs 20 to 25 to make. But they sell at Rs 140. So why would they remove that ban?' sighed Yenbaraj. 'If they remove the ban, everyone will benefit. I too will sell toddy, and everyone can split the profits. There is so much we can unlock if we remove this ban on toddy.'

Irudhayaraj and his family lived a short walk from Arul Yenbaraj's house. Apart from reaping the fruits borne by the tall palmyra tree in their backyard, they also raised hens and two goats. Irudhayaraj was ageing, but his muscles remained taut due to decades of climbing. 'If the government is to help us in any way, it should open toddy shops. But they won't because brandy godowns are all in the control of politicians. No point trusting the government,' Irudhayaraj said, his tone betraying that he had lost all hope. Every conversation I had with people in these regions took me by surprise, for their frankness and willingness to share. Here too, people were very keen to share their opinions and the stories of their lives with me.

The stories of their aspirations for their children were similar to those of the people in Vembar and Sayalgudi. 'My first son studied BCom and is looking for employment. My second son did not see any point in studying further. He said he is not going to get any job anyway and is working in a shop in Chennai. We intentionally didn't teach them how to climb. This is a difficult job; it is ceaseless. You can't sleep well for four to five months. Even if someone dies, you have to bury them and resume climbing the same day,' said Irudhayaraj.

This, to me, was the indication of a glaring paradox in contemporary education. At almost the precise moment when an increasing number of people who were formerly excluded from mainstream schooling come to recognize the empowering possibilities of education, many of the opportunities for these groups to benefit from schooling are disappearing.[10]

A generalization of the term 'education' and the supposed benefits one attained from it had served to mask how different enabling structures—access to economic capital, social linkages, gender and caste structures, and ascriptive identities—had all played a role in what education meant to the newer generation.

The conversations with these climbers indicated that the notion of 'getting educated' obscured the process of how one could actually get secure work and challenge social structures and institutions. It was as if sending the child to school or college would solve everything. Some people like Irudhayaraj's son felt that there was nothing to gain from getting educated. He saw that the promise of education was very much going unfulfilled.

None of Arul Yenbaraj's three children are now in the profession nor can they be, because they weren't taught to climb when they were young. 'We all work in construction now. There is a stable income there. But the cement makes our feet smooth, and this makes it difficult to climb trees,' said Arul.

Some other climbers I had spoken to mentioned with pride that their children were now in different engineering colleges. In Tamil Nadu, engineering colleges are rarely out of the news. In 2000, the number of private engineering colleges was around 100; by 2005, the number had hit 240, and by 2010, there were 526 private engineering colleges.[11] Since that time and after, technical education has come to completely dominate the discussion and perception of a valuable higher education in Tamil Nadu. According to C. J. Fuller and Haripriya Narasimhan,[12] one crucial reason why the number of engineering colleges has expanded so

quickly and why they are so politically important in Tamil Nadu—
as well as in the other southern states like Telangana, Andhra
Pradesh and Karnataka—is that they produce a vast majority
of graduates who make up the workforce of a rapidly growing
information technology (IT) sector. Many of these colleges are
horribly mismanaged, and the lack of quality is glaring.

Fuller and Narasimhan's research found that most IT
professionals within large IT companies belonged to urban
middle-class families, predominantly Brahmin or dominant
caste, despite the reservations policy that was in place for many
years in Tamil Nadu. They theorized that the reason for this
phenomenon is that these urban middle-class students are
likely to possess the communication skills (read good English)
needed to land these jobs. In other words, these graduates
have the social and cultural capital required for success in top
companies' selection procedures, something that had long been
denied to palmyra tree climbers. Geetha Nambissan highlighted
that a hard focus on English medium education, training in
math and science and access to coaching centres among other
market-based inputs are considered to be essential components
for school success in India.[13] This form of education was also
mostly concentrated towards the urbanized 'middle class' who
dominated the thinking on what education should and shouldn't
be. Geetha Nambissan also notes that these strategies and
practices of middle-class factions have led to the rapid growth
of the unregulated private sector in education, which was
exploiting the aspirations, anxieties and helplessness of families
belonging to the lower tiers of society.[14]

What is of concern is that sections of the poor or working
classes today are seeking 'quality education' for their children in
English-medium schools, and the unregulated private sector sees
this as a business opportunity. While it is beyond the scope of this
chapter to consider the acute shortcomings of schools and the

higher education sector in Tamil Nadu, it is evident that people like Anthony and Arul Yenbaraj were facing the repercussions of it. It didn't take long for the dignity associated with increased access to education to unravel into the indignity of unemployment and unemployability, which further compounded the difficulties of being a palmyra tree climber

The National Skill Development Corporation (NSDC), in its skill gap study for the state of Tamil Nadu, found negative semi-skilled and skilled labour requirements in agriculture, indicating that there is more supply than demand for agricultural labour.[15] In contrast, it logged a huge semi-skilled and skilled labour requirement in construction, tourism and travel, IT and in banking, financial services and insurance (BFSI). As per the report, this negative labour requirement in agriculture indicates that graduates, upon completing their school education, are going back to agriculture or are not accessing higher education and are sticking to agriculture. The skill gap in sectors like construction, tourism, IT and BFSI also indicates the lack of employability amongst graduates in Tamil Nadu. NSDC noted that skill sets do not match educational attainment, a certificate or degree does not necessarily signal the possession of particular skills, though it is meant to. But engineering colleges, like much of higher education in Tamil Nadu, offered the promise of some dignity, which people belonging to oppressed caste backgrounds saw as an opportunity of accessing higher education and potentially getting 'dignified' white-collar jobs. As the NSDC report seems to suggest, it has remained just a promise.

* * *

Before going to Vembar and Mukkudal, I was at election rallies in the run-up to the 2021 Tamil Nadu Legislative Assembly elections. People here were impatient and the politicians appeared nervous. Tamil Nadu is the second-largest economy in India after Maharashtra,[16] and yet everywhere I travelled with politicians, even in what was considered the affluent western districts of the states such as Erode, Coimbatore and Salem, the narrative of 'no jobs' was prevalent. The state was growing year on year, its Gross State Domestic Product (GSDP) increasing at a rate faster than the rate at which the country was growing,[17] but this was growth that was being cornered by a few. Jobs were scarce, and as mentioned earlier, more students were enrolling in higher education, but their employability was in question. Palmyra tree climbing could be lucrative, but lack of government recognition, a ban on tapping toddy, caste-based discrimination, and poor quality of education despite higher access to it, among other factors, were pulling these climbers into a vortex that appeared inescapable.

A Lok Sabha member of Parliament of the DMK was all set to campaign for the 2021 Tamil Nadu Legislative Assembly elections in a constituency called Omalur, in the district of Salem. He was weaving his day through a series of public talks there. This was a high-stakes election, a do-or-die situation for the DMK, who had been out of power for almost ten years. I was travelling with the MP at that time, helping design and organize his campaign. The palmyra tree climbers in Omalur had demanded an interaction with the MP, and this had been arranged by the local DMK leaders. A huge colourful temporary structure was set up in the middle of a palmyra tree plantation. Speakers blared songs glorifying the achievements of the leaders of the DMK, while over 500 climbers and their families patiently sat, waiting for the MP to arrive.

When we did arrive, there was no fanfare. The lack of enthusiasm was a telling sign, and the mood was suggestive of frustration and resentment. The climbers had had enough of politicians and the government. The MP climbed on the stage set up for him and greeted the gathering with joined palms, eliciting no response.

The event was meant to be a townhall, where the palmyra tree climbers would air their grievances and the leader would convey these grievances to the party high command, in the hope that if the party was elected, the government would be able to alleviate some of these grievances. The MP was introduced with multiple superlatives and honorifics to the sullen-faced climbers. They were impatient to speak.

Finally, one man stood up and introduced himself as someone who had done a PhD on palmyra trees and explained the multiple fallacies of governmental policy on palmyra trees. He introduced a palmyra tree climber next. He was clearly in the prime of his tree-climbing days, a fact that his ripped, bulky muscles suggested. He wore the colours of the DMK, red and black, and had a climbing harness around his shoulder. He took the mic and looked straight into the MP's eyes. 'Sir, if the government can make whiskey and brandy and sell to the people at an enormous profit, why can't we sell toddy to people around us? Is it because we are of a lower caste?' It was a startling question; it was showing truth to power.

I looked at the MP. He sat stone-faced and still. He knew that there was nothing he could say. Perhaps, the palmyra tree climbers had realized that there was no shortcut to empowerment, not even education. Empowerment had to take some local cultural form to have relevance, not a globalized form, and for them, it was toddy, a cultural form that was looked down upon by other cultures within the same state. Licensing the sale of this liquor would improve the earnings of the climbers manifold, exactly how it had happened in Kerala. But this was, of course, a politically unviable option.

An old man dressed in all white took the mic. 'This is the only job we know. *Enn thirudrenga,* Why are you stealing it from us?' he said to loud cheers and applause from the crowd.

The MP did what he could, promised to take these grievances to the leader and promised a better future when the DMK came to power. The climbers probably didn't expect anything else. Perhaps they just wanted to vent, to navigate possible futures that were not imposed on them by the state or society. Two years later, the government did stand up to some of its promises. A welfare board for palmyra tree climbers was instituted with a sitting MLA as a chairman.[18] The government was also encouraging innovation by investing in research to build palmyra tree climbing machinery. But the politics remain, and so does the caste-based discrimination.

For equitable redistribution of resources, the palmyra tree climbers wanted to be recognized, for their labour and for what they produce, to establish equality in how their status in society was perceived. Their claim was that this recognition would do what education was not doing; it would award some respect and establish a legacy of acknowledgement. Recognition played a crucial role—in the days I spent in Vembar and Mukkudal, and the year I spent travelling in Tamil Nadu on the campaign trail, I was continuously recognized as the *Padicha Thambi* (Educated Young Man) or *Veveram Sollra Thambi* (the young man who gave information) and often to everyone's amusement (including mine), *Vella Thambi* (Fair-Skinned Young Man). That recognition gave me capital that I could use, and I sensed that this was what palmyra tree climbers were asking for as well.

Back in Mukkudal, Yenbaraj took some loose tobacco from his wife, who was rolling it into beedis, and rolled one for himself. 'None of our children should get into this profession. They will be unemployed for eight months. What will these kids do for those eight months? They will all end up at the TASMAC every day,' said Yenbaraj. 'Let this profession die with us. But it is a good profession; you can make money.'

It appeared that these palmyra tree climbers were tired of the indignity of their work, an indignity that arose from their labour not being recognized, from the promise of education not being fulfilled, with most of their children unable to secure white-collar jobs that seemed to be the marker for dignity. The politics of globalization, which standardized education and pathways to success did not account for the palmyra tree climbers and their aspirations. They wanted a change from it all and saw education as a front to break away from social and economic hierarchies imposed upon them. But even accessing education didn't seem to suffice, for it wasn't a highway to better jobs and status. Their labour was still perilous, their identities still undignified and the rewards insufficient. Their identities and how people viewed them within a caste hierarchy didn't radically change just because the current generation was more educated. It was perhaps in this context that Rajesh said, 'Palmyra trees are our education.' At least, the trees held immediate potential for them to earn more and secure better futures.

Chapter 4

To Enter Entrance Exams

'The fortunate person is seldom satisfied with the fact of being fortunate. Beyond this, he needs to know that he has a right to his good fortune. He wants to be convinced that he deserves it and, above all, that he deserves it in comparison with others. He wishes to be allowed the belief that the less fortunate also merely experience their due.'

—Max Weber[1]

Retiring rooms at railway stations in India are an undiscovered comfort. For people used to hotels, the retiring room can be an abomination; the railways' legacy of carrying millions of people and the associated reputation of a lack of hygiene precedes it. But these retiring rooms are a well-kept secret; they are very well maintained, with clean sheets and clean bathrooms and are available at a fraction of the price of a hotel.

Most of these retiring rooms are on the first floor of the railway station, the staircase to it mostly lies in plain sight, but the millions of passengers passing by it every day tend to ignore it, their next destination beckoning. But when you stay on the first floor of a railway station, you can stand on the balcony overlooking the entrance and watch the hundreds and thousands of people enter and exit, each caught up in their own agendas, most in a hurry, some lost.

The view from the retiring room in Kota, Rajasthan, was sprawling; the station had a huge entrance flanked by banners containing photos of teenagers who had cracked the notoriously difficult IIT-JEE or NEET, entrance exams to the country's premier higher education institutes, and the institute that helped them crack it.

Every morning, I stood on the balcony with a cup of instant coffee and watched students and parents frantically enter and exit the station. It was something I enjoyed doing. I had once undergone the pressure of writing these exams myself, and now I could watch them from my ivory tower, observing and understanding, invisible to the people below me. Once you reach the platforms, you can hear the public announcement system blaring the names of multiple coaching institutions along with the area of the city they are located in. There are small TV screens that indicate the coach number on the platform and they also repeatedly play advertisements of coaching centres. Not for nothing is Kota considered the coaching capital of India. One of the largest coaching centres in Kota even broke the Guinness world record for 'the most number of students enrolled in one institution in one city', with a staggering 1.25 lakh enrolments in its Kota centre alone.[2] It can be extrapolated that around 2,50,000 students aged between fifteen to eighteen live in Kota year after year, preparing for multiple entrance exams, including the Joint Entrance Exam (JEE), though there is no official data or any form of regulation yet covering such a large interest group. Given that the total population of the town is about 1.5 million, this statistic is significant indeed.[3]

Every year around 1.1 to 1.3 million students[4] write the fiercely competitive entrance exam to India's premier technology institutes—the IITs. This exam and the institutes themselves have been subjects of much praise, prestige, criticism and research over the last few decades. There are twenty-three Indian Institutes of Technology (IIT) in India today. The seven older ones are IIT Bombay, Madras, Kharagpur, Kanpur, Roorkee, Guwahati and Delhi, which are the institutes of choice for every candidate. Roughly 17,000 seats are available every year within the IITs for the one million students whose dreams, efforts and sacrifices are put to the test through the JEE.[5]

Today, the JEE comprises two parts. The JEE Mains is the qualifying exam that every student writes and whose score is also considered for admission to multiple other engineering institutes across India. From the 1.5 million, 1,00,000 to 2,00,000 students qualify for the JEE-Advanced, from which the top 17,000 get admission to the IITs. Over the years, many of these candidates have come from one of the many coaching institutes in Kota. It is estimated that the coaching centres alone make a turnover of around more than Rs 1500 crore every year.[6] The town of Kota has come to signify coaching. Banners announcing a particular institute's performance in the JEE, large mugshots of JEE toppers and announcements of entrance tests to enter these coaching institutes adorned not just the train platforms but also on hoardings at highways and roads inside the city.

I exited the station and asked for directions to a bus stand that would take me to the coaching centres. I was told to go to Mahaveer Nagar, for that's where the 'big institutes' were. A cloud of dust welcomed me as I got off a rickety bus at Mahaveer Nagar in Kota, right in the middle of the road.

On either side of the road stood massive buildings, going up to what looked like at least twenty to thirty floors. A large mall came into view in the distance as the cloud of dust settled. I kept walking, a little apprehensive of navigating such wide roads and large buildings on foot. Unsure of what it was until I came to its entrance, I walked past one large complex that turned out to be the campus of one of the more prominent IIT-JEE coaching institutes in Kota. A coaching institute with a campus!

On the road adjacent to this behemoth of a building was a group of auto drivers, continuously beckoning me to take a ride with them. The complex in itself stood unassumingly, its facade wholly covered in glass, with some brown tiles for accent. Anyone unfamiliar with Kota and its legacy could have easily mistaken it for an office of a large multinational corporation.

It was clear that the economy of Kota depended a great deal on these coaching centres. Everyone in Kota, it seemed, had a stake in the coaching centres, small or big. The road adjacent to the massive complex had small tin shacks selling stationery and notebooks. A closer look at the shacks revealed that they were selling huge spiral-bound notebooks for students to practice their math, physics and chemistry problems. A little further down stood what I would call a giant bazaar catering to students' needs. There were stores offering to print out online forms for a rupee, mobile phone shops offering prepaid/postpaid recharges, tempered glasses to protect screens, wireless earphones and the like. Just a little beyond these shops were more stationery stores that stood next to each other jostling for the tiny space that was available. The road I had got off on was wide and flanked by large buildings with massive boundary walls. But these smaller arterial roads were a beehive of activity. The only adults on these roads were shop owners or shop helpers. The street was full of teenagers, many young boys sporting the beginnings of a moustache, walking purposefully to their destination—maybe to their next class or back to their accommodation to prepare for a test later in the evening.

While there was a thriving economy catering to every student's need, there was an even more prominent real estate economy, catering to what I imagine was housing for the hundred thousand teenagers who came to live in Kota. A short drive down the streets of Mahaveer Nagar, where a majority of the students in Kota lived and studied, indicated the sheer magnitude and complexity of the real estate scene there.

Massive apartments stood imposingly, rising up to dizzying heights. They were equipped with amenities such as swimming pools and gyms. On the same road stood small, old bungalows with decrepit signs reading 'Paying Guest Allowed, Only Girls' or 'Paying Guests Wanted, Boys Only'. Some other structures sported bright red banners claiming to be 'luxury boys' hostel'. These accommodations catered, I learnt, to the hundreds of smaller institutes. Some of the larger institutes had constructed enormous hostels next to their equally enormous buildings. One such hostel, aptly named 'Achievers Abode', advertised fully furnished AC rooms, biometric attendance, round-the-clock safety and even a diesel-generated power backup so that power cuts weren't an excuse to stop studying.

'When I first came to Kota, I struggled a bit. I barely knew Hindi, and 70 per cent of the classes in Kota are taken in Hindi, even in the English-medium batches,' chuckled Avinash, a young IITian who had been living and studying in Kota for two years before cracking the JEE and enrolling in a BTech course at IIT-Madras. I met him at IIT's sprawling, green campus when he was just about to graduate. He appeared relaxed and confident and was happy to recollect his experiences at Kota from a few years ago. 'It took a while to get accustomed to Kota, but you also have no choice other than getting accustomed to it. The good thing was I knew the basics of whatever they were teaching, and that was taught in English. But I wasn't really able to get hold of the explanation and the details,' (which were taught in Hindi) Avinash continued in a matter-of-fact way, which I later understood was the overall attitude of everyone I met in Kota. Avinash's grasp of the 'basics' was the starting point to developing a better understanding of a deep system that revolved around an examination like the JEE.

To grasp the 'basics', one is required to develop an acumen for math and science from a young age; concepts in these subjects were scaffolded rigorously for many students across the country as early as Grade 5. Students need appropriate training from that age to be able to grasp the depth and complexities of the JEE syllabus. If you didn't receive that training, you were likely to fall behind in the race, and like in any race, a strong head start always makes a difference.

Avinash was a rising cricketer when he was younger; the remnants of his athletic build were still present when I met him. He was now a tall and muscular young man with a neatly groomed beard and piercing eyes. 'The uncertainty of sport was too much for my parents and me. That's when I started going to math classes, and I found that I actually really liked math. When I started performing well in Grades 9 and 10, my teachers in school suggested I prepare for IIT-JEE, and that's how it started.'

Avinash wrote entrance exams to enter some coaching institutes. But he was unhappy with the peer group, which he described as 'uncompetitive'. Throughout 2016, he went to a premier coaching institute in Chennai and then to one in Bangalore. At the all-India entrance test conducted by the coaching institute in Kota, he was one of the top rankers in the South India zone and was then asked to join their Kota institute. A few trial classes at Kota convinced him of the faculty's competencies and also of his peers' 'competitiveness'.

Excellent private schooling, supportive and wealthy parents and his grasp of 'basics' allowed Avinash to pursue steadfastly what was only an aspirational pipedream for the million-odd students who appeared for the JEE each year. The exam tested the notions of what every Indian thought of as success and how to achieve it.

Avinash soon moved to Kota from Chennai in late 2016 with his mother, and they took up a rented accommodation in one of the larger apartments. In the two years that he was there, his day was well structured and regimented. The morning was dedicated to self-study and completing Daily Practice Papers (DPPs). Classes started from 2 p.m. and went on till 8 p.m. Avinash's mother had the luxury of working from home, so she would work and ensure he got all his meals on time and that his health and nutrition were taken care of. This privilege makes a huge difference, as the owner of one of the more prominent coaching institutes told me.

'Most of the students who come to Kota have a strong grasp of basics. Many of them had probably joined a coaching institute in Grade 6 or 7. It is really important,' Avinash emphasized. There were students as young as 5th and 6th graders (ten and eleven-year-old children) living full-time in Kota now. 'In fact, there was this friend of mine who came to Kota two years before me. He was attending "foundation" classes and JEE classes. But he wasn't with his mother, and he wasn't very focused. He used to roam around a lot and go to gaming centres and malls. When he came to Grade 11, and JEE preparations started picking up, he couldn't perform well and meet his parents' or the faculty's expectations. He wasn't able to build on the weak foundation. The transition is very difficult once you go down that line.'

Discipline was important, and so was docility. Everyone was supposed to follow the same routine—eat and sleep at specified times, study at the specified hours and if allowed, play occasionally. It gave parents a sense of security that their child was not going to go wayward; it gave centre owners the satisfaction that a large number of students were under their control, an illusion that they were providing the same, equal opportunities to all. When someone was unable to reconcile with docility, the ecosystem worked well to shut them out.

Ajantha Subramanian, a Harvard anthropologist, noted in *Caste of Merit*[7] that caste and class history were the key to examination success in the JEE and the rank that one secured there. And, indeed, Avinash is a case in point. It became apparent soon enough to me that the people who could come to Kota and avail the services of these coaching institutes were from a financially sound background, something that is a marker of the more privileged castes.

Within this bastion of privilege and superior access lay an invisibilization of the very privilege that got these students here. These institutes worked within the realm of being completely objective, going only by the performance of the student and nothing else. But through my interactions with students, faculty and the owners of these coaching institutes, I could see that this emphasis on excellence intentionally papered over the very crucial point that caste and class history played a key role in examination success.

The notions of excellence and competitiveness sometimes manifested in an extreme manner. Avinash told me of a common practice that happened within the institutes—sorting!

Since Avinash had scored very high in the entrance exam held by the coaching institute, he was assigned to the 'star' batch, whereas many other students were assigned to 'normal' batches. But it didn't end there. One had to continue to perform well in the various tests to remain in the 'star' batch.

'When I first joined the star batch, the faculty wasn't pleased with me. They said if I didn't perform well in the next two tests, I would be sent to the normal batch. But luckily, I did pretty well, and I continued in the star batch,' Avinash said, his voice betraying a hint of pride. Some institutes conducted exams every year to shuffle students, and some conducted them every month to reassign students to the batches that fit their skill sets well at the moment. The narrative was always, 'If you work hard and excel, you can get to the star batch'.

'Initially, the opinion of the faculty was that I wouldn't last in the star batch for more than ten days, and I would be back home in Tamil Nadu within a couple of weeks. That's the level of competition that these institutes prepare you for,' Avinash continued.

'What is so different about the star batch as compared to the normal batches?' I asked Avinash.

'Well, to start with, the star batch has only ten students, whereas normal batches can have up to 120 students. It is the batch for people who can prospectively get very high ranks in the JEE,' Avinash chuckled. 'The faculty in the star batch are also very experienced and, more importantly, dig deep into the concepts. In the normal batch, they don't really dig that deep because students might find it difficult to grasp such concepts. Instead, they give a lot more problems to solve, or they teach by examples.'

The sorting, based on continuously evaluating the performance of these teenagers, all to create an atmosphere of competition, even manifested in the kind of accommodation these children could live in.

A cursory reading of the website of one of the largest institutes in Kota revealed even more about the intricacies of sorting.

One such scheme was the Kohinoor Hostel Scheme, which was run by one institute. The claim was that this institute provided a real competitive environment exclusively for topper students by providing accommodation facilities in spacious, fully furnished hostels equipped with 'academic amenities'. It also promised that students would be mentored regularly by the director and faculty members.

Further, based on students' ranks in particular tests, the scholarship criteria were fixed for students taking up this accommodation. Below is a screenshot of how the scholarship was decided.

CUMM. RANK	SCHOLARSHIP AMOUNT*
Rank 01	Rs. 5000/-
Rank 02 to 05	Rs. 4000/-
Rank 06 to 10	Rs. 3000/-
Rank 11 to 20	Rs. 2000/-
Rank 21 to 50	Rs. 1000/-
Rank 51 to 100	Allowed to continue in hostel
Above 100	May be asked to vacate the hostel

These were hostels of 'excellence' where the best performers stayed together. The message was that if you slipped to a rank below 100, you didn't belong there any more. Students had to continuously compete to be allowed to even stay in such places. To these institutes, nurturing students involved creating an atmosphere of intense competition.

Competitions needed to reward participants as well. The select few who were able to secure top ranks in the JEE were the poster children of all the coaching institutes. Giant banners featuring their faces, signatures and ranks could be found everywhere—highways, bus stops, at the entrances of coaching institutes and even in a small poster I found stuck inside a restaurant's washroom. This wasn't a phenomenon exclusive to just Kota. This was seen everywhere in the country. It was emblematic of what happens across India. The very few who rise to the top are hero-worshipped, and the hundreds of millions are made to look at them in awe—the very few smart and the very many dumb.

When institutes didn't necessarily produce toppers in a particular year, they chose to co-opt.

Manish Gupta (name changed) was one such curious case. In 2021, he secured a top all-India rank in the JEE. I woke up, still sleepy, one hazy October morning in Delhi after an exhausting trip to Kota, and opened the newspaper to find a full front-page advertisement by a top IIT-JEE coaching institute. The advertisement had information on Manish's rank, the course he had taken at the coaching institute and a handwritten testimonial with his signature. Above his face in the advertisement was a bold proclamation: 'All India Topper and Ranks 2 and 3 are students of our Classroom Programme. Total Domination—6 in top 10, 12 in top 20'. The advertisement continued on the next page, with comprehensive details about the coaching institute's upcoming 'talent hunt' with scholarships worth crores.

The narrative of domination and conquest notwithstanding, I found this rather curious because I had seen a similar ad on Facebook recently where his face and testimonial had been featured in an advertisement by another leading institute. In Kota itself, as I learnt later, a lot of people were talking about him. '*Manish ne toh kamaal kar diya* (Manish has created wonders),' said a man selling samosas in Kota. But surely, he couldn't have gone to two different institutes at the same time!

'This is a common phenomenon,' Avinash said, when I asked him about Manish being in multiple institutes. 'When I got into IIT, an institute I wrote an entrance exam for a few years ago approached me to feature my face on their banner. They offered a "scholarship".' Scoring a high rank in the JEE made these students immediate and temporarily valuable commodities. It was their one shot at fame, and many gladly agreed to front multiple institutes. After all, they had established 'dominance' over a million other youngsters to get to where they were, and they felt that they deserved to have their moment in the sun. The days after the announcement of the JEE results saw the usual frenzied media activity of interviewing toppers. All the leading newspapers in India carried these interviews, which revealed the books they used, the institutes they went to, their preparation strategy and their future plans. And as the trend seemed to suggest, computer science at IIT-Bombay appeared to be the course and institute of choice.

The media frenzy with teenagers as brand ambassadors had created a more significant phenomenon. The number of students registering for JEE has increased year on year. When the JEE was first introduced in 1961, a few thousand students wrote it. Sixty years later, it has secured the reputation of being the 'do or die' exam for over 1.3 million students every year.

It was not just the students who had their time in the limelight, with their faces plastered across the country. 'Celebrity' and 'star' faculty also carried great value. They often turned out to be the clincher for anxious parents figuring out which coaching institute to invest lakhs in for their wards.

'Sir, faculty is everything. They are like God in Kota,' said an autorickshaw driver. Driving through Kota, one could see several banners displaying the faces of older Indian men sporting severe expressions. It was as if a smile would take away the seriousness of the JEE. I didn't spot a single woman on these banners.

Kota was not the only place with an abundance of coaching institutes. Hyderabad was another city where students and parents took entrance exams very seriously.

It was a humid, rainy day in Hyderabad. I was evading honking bikes, manoeuvring past people squirming for space among dingy buildings and searching for a coaching institute called Sparkle (name changed). Opposite a tea stall, a paan shop, and a bike garage stood a building complex, and on its second floor was a dingy and cramped coaching centre. The elderly owner, Kishore (name changed), was sitting nervously on his seat.

Kishore was a small man with a big grey beard, and he nervously kept tapping the floor with his feet. Enough had been written about the entrance exam coaching industry, and as it is, business for him was bad. His institute was not able to retain students, and when I went to meet him, there were about six or seven students crammed in a very small room. Perhaps, he thought that I was there to malign him. For every behemoth coaching centre such as Allen, Akash, Bansal and FIITJEE, a hundred other smaller ones offered a range of services that apparently the bigger ones wouldn't provide. Personalized attention and smaller classrooms were the biggest USPs of these smaller institutes, and Sparkle was one such. Kishore started speaking nervously with me, while a math class was going on in the next room.

His father had started one of the first coaching centres for entrance exams in India back in the 1960s, or so he claimed. The family had started off in one of their properties—a hundred-year-old building. In time, the coaching centre became very popular and had over a few thousand students. But in the 1990s, with India liberalizing and opening itself to private sector investment, the demand for engineering seats grew exponentially, and so did the demand for coaching institutes. It was around this time when the behemoth institutes established themselves.

Aakash and Allen opened in 1988, Bansal in 1991, FIITJEE in 1992 and Shri Narayana in 1999. This opened the floodgates for the coaching industry, but it also meant that many existing players who couldn't adapt got lost, and so did Kishore's father's business.

'I have been in this industry for more than forty years, Sir, let me tell you. Nothing matters more than the faculty. But with so many options now, they are spoilt for choice. No one is loyal any more,' sighed Kishore. 'As soon as they see someone is paying better, they immediately jump to that institute.' However, when the pandemic hit, many institutes that relied solely on physical classes immediately lost business. The pandemic happened too fast and too close to the JEE for them to adapt to online classes. While COVID-19 had wreaked havoc overall, the entrance exam coaching sector was one of the most affected sectors. Moreover, with lockdowns being enforced, many hostels and institutes had to be shut down as students, the mainstay of the Kota economy, left en masse for their homes. '*Bahut buri haalat ho gayi* (The situation turned very bad),' a shopkeeper explained to me.

Many of the faculty members I spoke to in Kota mentioned that they hadn't been paid in months, but none wanted to go on record. Considering such precarious circumstances, Kishore was quite proud to announce that he had paid all his faculty regularly and on time. 'That's why they are not leaving me now,' he said, looking content with himself. With his son joining the business, a fresh perspective allowed the institute to survive. It adapted to the pandemic by quickly starting a YouTube channel and training the faculty to use online tools to teach. With this technology, he claimed that students didn't have to move to Hyderabad to study. They could sit in their homes wherever they were and prepare.

'I don't have star faculty; they are all in the grasp of the bigger institutes in Hyderabad, such as the Narayanas and the Chaitanyas,' said Kishore, in a matter-of-fact way, referring to the top institutes. The presence of star faculty also fuelled the ambitions of the institute. The coaching institutes with the best and the most reputed faculty could aim for top ranks in the JEE. Some institutes that only had a few faculty members would aim to get their students into IITs. Everyone else came up with their own notions of success and acted accordingly. Kishore and his son were quite clear that their focus was to get their students into NITs and into 'decent' colleges within Telangana. Such a thought would be considered heresy in Kota. With star faculty, institutes also had the licence to charge fees the way they saw fit. While Kishore deemed it fit to charge around Rs 30,000 for a year-long course, the bigger institutes charged anywhere between Rs 1,00,000 to 4,00,000 for a year, with further 'non-refundable costs' on things such as books and uniforms. Today, institutions such as the Narayana Group have over 750 schools, colleges and coaching centres across twenty-three states in India, employing 50,000 teachers.[8]

The coaching industry now functions as a free market, susceptible to the vagaries of demand and supply—both of which are only growing. If the JEE was meant to be an exam to help the best students in India get the best technical education, the inability to afford good-quality coaching acts as an entry barrier. Over and above that, every coaching institute has entrance tests like the one Avinash wrote.

Today, these entrance tests to the coaching institute are administered at an all-India level and conducted in over 300 cities and towns throughout India. One's performance in this test determines one's batch (like Avinash's star batch and the normal batch) and also what kind of faculty one has. If there were five to six star faculty members in an institute, one could access them only based on exceptional performance in the entrance tests. To perform well in these tests, one needed good schooling, good nutrition, supportive parents and a good socio-economic background. Did these entrance exams, therefore, reflect natural ability or socially reproduced cultural capital?

The former chief economic adviser of India, Arvind Subramanian, and an economist at Pennsylvania State University, Rohit Lamba, analysed data from the Government of India's National Family Health Survey (NFHS). This data was collected from all four surveys that were conducted (1992, 1998, 2005 and 2015). In their study, they found that at least in terms of educational quantities (not necessarily in terms of quality), i.e., number of years of schooling, Hindu upper-caste children were converging with developed-country averages at almost twelve years of schooling. The education gap, in terms of the number of years of education children receive, has shrunk somewhat between the upper-caste Hindus and the other backward castes (from 1.8 years in 1998 to 1.4 years in 2015), the scheduled castes (from 2.9 years in 1998 to 2.4 years in 2015), and scheduled tribes (from 3.8 years in 1998 to 3.5 years in 2015). However, it has widened for Muslims (from 2.6 years in 1998 to 3.1 years in 2015). The researchers concluded that while other groups are catching up with dominant castes, it is slow for many groups and almost absent for Muslims.[9]

The fact that members of dominant castes have a significant two to three years more of schooling as compared to other socio-economic groups in India indicates broad patterns of continuing inequality in educational outcomes. Samarth Bansal and Pramit Bhattacharya analysed unit-level data from ASER (Annual Survey of Education Report—one of India's most extensive surveys measuring educational outcomes) and showed that household characteristics shape learning outcomes of children much more than the type of school children attend. They found that 72 per cent of highly privileged children between Class 3 and 5 could read a Class 1 text while only 33.55 per cent of underprivileged children between Class 3 and 5 could read a Class 1 text. They also found that underprivileged children with barely educated parents learn the least. This also means that children from underprivileged families can rise above the station of their birth only if they are lucky to be born to well-educated parents.[10]

Clearly, these have ramifications on who writes the JEE and who has access to these coaching institutes. Interestingly, the 49th IIT council met on 6 October 2015 and decided to form a committee of eminent persons to review the current JEE system for admission into IITs.[11]

The report of the committee noted that 'the current coaching is a very lucrative "industry" . . . it has revenues of approximately Rs 24,000 crores per year. However, it seems to fill a void—the absence of good teaching in schools—and does it effectively enough to make lots of money also.' The committee had three objections, however:

- The first is philosophical (yet important). The purpose of education is refinement of the mind, not passing an entrance examination.

- The second concerns the fact that all work and no play makes a 12th-grade student a dull individual with less involvement in activities other than studies.
- The third is that students are forced to waste a lot of time commuting to avail the benefit of 'good' coaching.[12]

While the objections could be valid, the committee in no way considered the broadening inequalities in educational outcomes and their effects on India's favourite political debate: meritocracy. The evidence pointed out by Arvind Subramanian, Rohit Lamba and multiple other scholars and data journalists shows that unequal access to learning continues to be an instrument of elite dominance, and the JEE supports that. These entrance exams, among other things, reflected the committee's preference for students who followed rules, accepted authority and were reliable and precise, which were the demands of a globalized, homogeneous workforce.

On the flip side, Harvard professor and anthropologist Ajantha Subramanian notes that with the abundance of coaching institutes, more and more students who might have previously thought the IITs out of their reach have turned to Kota and Hyderabad in hopes of admission.

All of the above data analysis is not just a critique of coaching institutes but an understanding of the structure of an exam like the JEE. Noted sociologist Satish Deshpande highlights that examinations that entail such heavy pressure as the JEE are forced to conflate eligibility with excellence because of the gatekeeping function they have to perform.[13]

Today, there exist plenty of websites on the Internet that allow you to predict what rank one will get based on their aggregate marks in the JEE. Borrowing from Satish Deshpande's framework, the top ranker in JEE Mains in 2021 was expected to score between 291 and 300 marks, whereas the 4000th ranker was expected to score between 207 and 209 marks. A mere 91 marks divided 4000 people, which means 43 students per mark.[14]

A rank in the top 100 as opposed to the top 5000 made a world of difference to a candidate. 'If I hadn't made it within the top 200, I wouldn't have been able to get into the course of my choice. Beyond the top few hundred ranks, people have to choose whatever course they get at whichever IIT,' Avinash said. Through such microscopic ranking, the JEE claimed to measure merit as if saying that the person who got 288 marks in the JEE and the person who got 275 were vastly different and deserved wholly different fates.

The bigger coaching institutes in Kota have come to understand the significance of every mark and have built elaborate software to track performance, suggest strategies to improve performance in particular areas and also predict the JEE rank by considering the current level of the student. Students write all-India tests with students of all other branches of their particular institute to understand where they stand currently, and the software then gives them detailed analyses vis-à-vis other students' performances.

The report of the committee to examine the JEE system recommended that the union government introduce a new system of examinations in 2017 by setting up a National Testing Service agency, similar to the one in the US, which would conduct an aptitude test. It further recommended that this aptitude test be developed so that it is 'independent of coaching'. As this book is published, this report continues to sit on the ever-growing list of discarded or ignored recommendations to reform education and examinations in India.

Avinash regularly scored in the top fifty ranks in the all-India tests conducted by his institute. He was told that it is generally expected that his rank in the JEE would be three times the rank he was scoring in the institute All-India tests. 'My target was to be in the top 100 in India in JEE, but no matter how hard I tried, I couldn't cross the 50 barrier in the all-India tests, and the faculty weren't able to figure out why either. So, I had to make peace with the fact that I would probably get within the top 200 in the JEE,' Avinash said.

The week before the JEE, Avinash decided to keep it really simple. He didn't attempt any new difficult questions. He just practised a few problems that had appeared in previous years' papers and ensured he didn't look at any questions that would make him doubt his abilities. 'A few days of last-minute preparation was not going to take over the three years of effort I had put into this,' he reasoned. But Avinash couldn't write the exam in Kota as he couldn't get a seat in any examination centre there. So, he had to travel to Delhi. The day before the exam, he took a train with his mother to Delhi.

The day of the exam arrived. It was the day when a test of a few hours would impact the fortunes of hundreds of thousands of children across India. It was now a rite of passage for millions of students. Avinash went in confidently and did what he had been doing for three years every day—solve problems and mark the correct answer out of multiple choices on a sheet.

A couple of months passed in anxiety as one's fate dangled in the air. It is this period when most mentally exhausted students take a break and completely relax, for there is nothing to do but wait for the results.

Just as the day of the exam came, the day of the results crept in unassumingly. For the world, it was yet another day. For Avinash, it was the day that would decide which IIT he would be in and which course he would get, a decision that had multiple social, economic and cultural ramifications.

He had secured the 180th rank amongst the 1.2 million students who wrote it that year. The prediction of his institute was almost entirely accurate. His rank was about three times that of his rank in the all-India tests conducted by the institute. The marks he scored in the JEE were five to ten marks less than the people who came in the top 100.

Far away in Hyderabad, Suhasini was distraught because of her results. The rank she scored was not enough to get her into any IIT. Left with no apparent choice, she enrolled in the Sparkle repeater batch to give it another go. But this time, her parents' and her goals had slightly changed. She was happy to get into an IIT/IIIT or an NIT within her home state.

The repeater batch consisted of other students like her, young seventeen or eighteen-year-olds giving the JEE one more try. The pale Hyderabad sun filtered its way into the dingy classroom where a class in physics was going on. Suhasini paid attention to it keenly, the fear of not getting through in her second attempt bearing heavily on her mind.

Fiercely competitive exams like the JEE peddled the narrative of meritocracy, that the exam 'levelled the playing field' and was the 'fairest' way to ensure that only the most meritorious got into the hallowed portals of the IITs every year. But as the political philosopher Michael Sandel points out, one of the deeper flaws in the notion of meritocracy is that the qualities of a person considered meritorious and the talents valued by society are fundamentally down to random luck.[15] The random chance of being born into a supportive family, being in a location with good access to basic education and having some amount of privilege all play a role in ensuring this success. Exams like the JEE have fortified the belief that people who come out on top deserve their success, and those who fail deserve their fate. This, as Sandel points out, is the harsher side of meritocracy. It creates a politics of humiliation.

The large buildings and campuses of the coaching institutes in Kota slowly receded into the background as I left Mahaveer Nagar in an auto-rickshaw, back to my ivory tower at the railway station's retiring room.

'Sir, you know the biggest problem here in Kota?' asked the auto driver.

I looked back at him curiously.

'Sir, a lot of these children come here to study, but they end up getting a boyfriend or a girlfriend and don't study.'

Chapter 5

A Good Mother

'... *If you are not like everybody else, then you are abnormal; if you are abnormal, then you are sick. These three categories, not being like everybody else, not being normal and being sick, are in fact very different but have been reduced to the same thing.*'

—Michel Foucault[1]

'He would never sit down. It was a nightmare to even get him to sit in one place and feed him. He threw these crazy temper tantrums, and there was no way out,' said Gayathri (name changed) as we settled in to talk about Vidyut (name changed), her son. A few years ago, Vidyut had been diagnosed with attention-deficit/hyperactivity disorder (ADHD), which is characterized by a combination of poor attention, hyperactivity and impulsivity that is supposedly excessive for the child's developmental level and leads to impaired functioning.

'As he was growing up, around the age of three, my son stopped making eye contact, and his speech was very delayed. All he could say at that time was "yes" or "no".' Gayathri was a middle-aged mother based out of Chennai. Her husband had a travelling job and often had to go to the United States, so the sole responsibility of taking care of a child diagnosed with ADHD fell on Gayathri.

'By the time Vidyut was five, we had been in at least six cities,' said Gayathri, looking up to the ceiling, trying to remember the number of places they had shifted to. She was an ambitious woman who was doing well in her career, but her husband's job forced them to relocate multiple times.

'I started earning at the age of eighteen,' she smiled fondly. 'After having started working at a young age and also being a passionate engineer, I wanted to do an MBA and scale the corporate ladder,' she said, her face betraying her stoic position with respect to her unrealized dreams. 'Vidyut came into my world and changed it. Honestly, I will say for the better. He is my guiding light. There were a few red flags during my pregnancy itself, but we fought through all of it, and he was born in April 2009. There is one crucial thing that no mother has been educated about. Vidyut had a delayed birth cry. I didn't know it back then, but I learned later that if children have a delayed birth cry, there are chances that they will have delayed developmental milestones,' she said.

I looked back at her, slightly puzzled.

'You know, milestones such as the onset of speech, the ability to recognize words and interact with the world, etc. There are detailed descriptions on multiple websites as to when a child should do this, when a child should do that,' she said. Short-term implications for those diagnosed with ADHD included poor academic performance, disciplinary problems in the classroom, social ostracization and low self-esteem.

'The first red flag was when Vidyut was eighteen months old; he had delayed speech,' remembered Gayathri, now settling into sharing her story. 'I went to the doctor, and they were not perturbed at all. The doctor said this is normal; some children just speak late. I was the eldest in my family; I didn't have any nieces or nephews, so, I couldn't compare his development to that of any other child. I couldn't understand why my child was different.'

Her tone indicated there was a lot more to what she was actually saying. She sounded like she was blaming herself.

'For a really long time, I was not aware. I thought this was the way it goes,' said Vaishnavi (name changed) in a Zoom call from Erode, Tamil Nadu. She was a dentist and a mother of a child with ADHD and autism. The COVID-19 pandemic had not allowed us to interact in person. Even on the Zoom call, it was evident that Vaishnavi had a genial and calm demeanour. It was as if she was at peace with herself and her surroundings. 'When he was almost two, his regression started,' she said.

'What do you mean by regression?' I asked, curious to understand more about the term.

'Before that, his eye contact was very good. His socializing was also good then; he demanded a lot of attention as a small baby. Then, there was a drastic change in behaviour. When we lived abroad, socialization opportunities weren't as many as they were in India. I thought it was because of that, and if we exposed him to more people, he would be better. All my friends' kids, three to four kids of the same age, had pacifiers, but he wouldn't use them. He was not accepting of routine change; he would only eat when my household help would feed him. Sometimes, I had to force-feed him,' she recounted.

Here too, the mother had to be responsible for multiple things, not just for taking care of the child's daily needs but also for being responsible for the child's behaviour and development. As a practising dentist, Vaishnavi was growing in her practice but soon had to give up her work. In both these cases, gender and, in particular, gendered roles in parenting seem to have had particularly damaging effects on the mothers of children diagnosed with ADHD.

'My son would barely sleep; he had so much energy in him. The energy would manifest in crying, tantrums or, sometimes, just running around the house. I remember that I slept a maximum of two hours a day for a few years. When I was working, I used to have a separate cabin. I used to take a power nap for fifteen minutes. That gave me some respite because I wasn't sleeping at all. I used to be scared of weekends because I wouldn't be able to sleep. I had to be prepared to engage the child. At home, I was fully dedicated to him. I was trying to compensate because of the guilt I had from being in the workplace while he was diagnosed with ADHD,' she said.

Mother-blaming is not a new phenomenon in any society, especially in a society like India, which has for long had very gendered and hierarchized notions of parenting. Vaishnavi and Gayathri's feelings of guilt and inadequacy perhaps came from a very gendered understanding of what it took to be a good mother. Decades of conditioning and fables of a mother's unconditional commitment and sacrifice bore heavily on them. Both of them were highly educated, one an engineer, with a promising corporate career, and the other a dentist, with a flourishing practice. Asking for unconditional commitment and sacrifice from such women often becomes equivalent to asking them to give up their careers.

'But who do you think demanded this sacrifice, the child or your husband or in-laws?' I asked.

Vaishnavi let out a mighty laugh. 'Let me tell you what happened when we first visited the paediatrician,' she said.

'During our first visit, he kept taking things from my handbag and flinging it across the clinic. The paediatrician said he had a developmental disorder and asked us to come back after a week because she was going on vacation.'

That night, Vaishnavi didn't sleep at all. A week was too long a wait, especially when she had been told that her son had a developmental disorder. Soon enough, a battery of tests and assessments were administered to her son. He was formally diagnosed with ADHD and autism, but the psychologist said it was mild to moderate.

Vaishnavi's son was prescribed a bunch of performance-enhancing drugs, three to four different kinds. 'They said it would calm him down,' she said. However, after a few days, Vaishnavi decided she didn't want to administer medicines to her child to change his behaviour.

'A bunch of people said he needs therapy, and I thought this was a much better idea,' she continued. 'My family, especially my husband and in-laws, was not supportive. I wanted to take him to Chennai, where I knew there were good facilities, but my family wanted to treat him in Coimbatore.' Between the visit to the first paediatrician and the assessment, in ten days, Vaishnavi had decided to quit her dentistry practice. She had first decided to take six months off, but the next day it became evident that a six-month sabbatical wasn't an option.

'I saw that being depressed was affecting my child. He used to come to me and pull my lips to make me smile,' she said, showing me how he would put his index fingers on either side of her lips and push them upward to make it look like she was smiling. 'That emotional bond was there. He could understand, but he was not able to articulate. That was the source of his frustration, and the temper tantrums began. Once he began speaking, you should have seen the confidence he had. It increased drastically. Once I realized my behaviour was affecting my child, I had to force myself to be happy. My job was gone, my dreams were gone, but I had to live in the present and be happy for my child.'

Vaishnavi, in her words, had more 'pressing concerns'; she had to take her child regularly for therapy to a different city as Erode didn't have the infrastructure for therapy and handling multiple questions about her child.

'Soon, my husband's side started making snide comments and asking us questions,' she recalled with a sigh. 'Both of them were working and that's why the child is having these issues. Why is she spending so much? The child will be fine. All of this is unnecessary; they are creating problems for themselves. Why does she have to go to Chennai? She thinks she knows everything.' These were some common refrains she grew accustomed to.

In any case, Vaishnavi packed her bags and moved to Chennai to commence her son's therapy. 'Initially, I stayed with some relatives and then I rented a house. There were financial issues, but my parents supported me. My father sold one of his properties, all for his grandchild. He was retired; he thought his daughter was settled in life, and he was in a happy place before I threw this bomb on him,' she laughed, but her laughter betrayed multiple emotions. Even on the call, there was a determination and desperation in her voice, and a large part of her seemed to be finding ways to negotiate an imposed guilt. I felt that she understood this was not her fault, but as a mother, she 'had to' shoulder the blame.

Her son's therapy began, and he was responding well, but her husband had lost his job during that time. 'He had his own issues to deal with, and he started taking it out on me,' she said. 'The way I see it, men are not trained to adapt to these changes. The husband is another child, but sometimes I feel my son is better because he at least responds,' she chuckled, as we both revelled in the lightness of that moment. But through all this, another responsibility was apparent to the mother: helping her husband understand.

Societal conditioning, questions, comments and the pressure of having to be answerable for the child would have severe effects on their marriage as well. 'I became very particular about who my husband was interacting with and meeting because he was getting influenced by everything he was listening to. When he was with a broad-minded group, he would also be broad-minded. But when he was not, he'd go back to being his conservative self,' she recollected, lost in thought.

'How has your husband's relationship with your child evolved?' I asked, now wary that I was treading into her personal space. But Vaishnavi was only too eager to share.

'My husband wanted his son to tell him that his father is the best, and he thought he could achieve that by giving. It was coming from a position of insecurity,' she continued, deep in thought.

The fact that he was away from his son during the day and that his wife was with his son continuously made him feel inadequate. 'He was very particular about sleeping in between the child and me. He wanted attention from the child as well,' Vaishnavi laughed out loud. For Vaishnavi's husband, the world seemed to exist only for him. That his wife was doing everything and beyond was almost invisible to him, his years of education and sound qualifications serving only as an eyewash to hide what was actually going on inside his head.

'A few years ago, when my son was still having difficulty with speech, my husband was yelling at me. It was something about me not having taken care of him properly. My son could understand everything that was happening; he was just not able to articulate a defence. He just dragged me out of the room, shut the door, sat me down on the sofa and lay on my lap,' she said, as a teardrop descended down her face. 'I was totally moved, and my husband was feeling really bad, but not because he understood what was happening, but because his son was taking his mother's side,' she declared. The weight of her words hung heavily in the air.

I was in a fix about what to say; on one hand, this was a story laden with subtext—one about the intelligence and agency of a child and how hierarchical and patriarchal norms affect parenting—and on the other hand, this was a deeply personal vignette of her relationship with her husband. Thankfully, she continued the conversation herself, sparing me the discomfort.

'Now, my son is seven years old, and his IQ is very high. He can read three languages, and he is wonderful at math. Every child has some talent somewhere; we just have to initiate it,' she said.

In a straitjacketed world of going after milestones and achievements, success for a parent like Vaishnavi or Gayathri meant something very different. These mothers played multiple roles—diet and homework supervisor, medicine administrator, occupational therapist, eye-exercise supervisor and even driver, amongst various other unrecognized and unsaid roles. Somewhere in between, they had to find ways to be themselves. It was evident that mothers like Vaishnavi had to continuously self-evaluate, not just about how her child was improving and responding to interventions, but also whether she was a good mother as prescribed by the discourses of motherhood. In between all of this, the idea of schooling and a formal education came in.

'I think it was 2017, if I remember right,' said Gayathri. 'The school Vidyut went to was a regular private CBSE school—you know one of the many you find in the suburbs of cities. They called me all of a sudden and said my son was urinating in class. But my son was potty trained, and also he was eight years old at that time; he had bladder control. So, I was taken aback; this had never happened before.'

A child urinating in class was sure to mess up interactions and create labels among young children. Gayathri was severely worried. Her son had just started to get better at speech and was slowly gaining confidence, making friends in this new school. It had been only three months since he had started in this school, and news of him urinating in class sent her into a tizzy.

'I went to the school, and the principal asked me to check if he had a urinary tract infection, but he was perfectly fine at home.' The school asked her to check what was happening and sent her back home with a warning that if this continued, they would be unable to keep him in the school. But it didn't stop. Vidyut seemed perfectly fine at home with his toilet habits. So, she went back to school and asked her son's class teacher about how children used the restroom.

The children were taken to the restroom during breaks by the cleaning staff, and one of the staff noticed that Vidyut would go to the restroom but never use it, and he would come back to class and relieve himself. Gayathri asked if she could see the restroom that her son was taken to. The restroom had only the Indian squatting type of commode, something Vidyut had never seen before and thus had no idea how to use it. In fear of embarrassing himself in the restroom, he never used it.

Gayathri immediately took her son to her father's house, which happened to have an Indian-style commode. Two days later, she stopped receiving these kinds of complaints.

'Every day, I send my child to school with the hope that today he can handle himself, that he has to. But you also have to be mentally prepared to deal with any situation that comes up. Obviously, I couldn't tell anyone else about this; imagine what would have happened to his self-esteem,' Gayathri said, the tears now flowing.

For many years, Vidyut's ADHD was quite challenging to handle; apart from hyperactivity and inattentiveness, he was unable to perform at school. Until the age of five, he was unable to even read a word. Teachers would sit with him through the day and use multiple techniques to get him to read, all for him to forget it immediately.

'I had to assume the role of a teacher; there was no choice. He had to prove to someone that he was capable of reading; otherwise, they would have put him in some special school, which would only affect him more. He is a perfectly normal child; he was just having difficulty retaining information,' she said.

Vidyut was able to trust only his mother; perhaps she never betrayed any sign of judgement and gave him all the love he needed to value himself as he grew up. Soon enough, with his mother's intensive coaching, he picked up reading.

'The support of the teacher is so important; teachers are like second parents. But I wouldn't blame any teacher particularly. They are handling a class of thirty to forty children. How can one teacher manage?' she said.

'How do you handle this label, that your son has ADHD, is hyperactive, has a learning disorder and all that?' I asked.

'In almost every school I put him, he was labelled "special". The word "special" definitely puts pressure on the mother. It makes you feel guilty. I often wonder what I have done wrong to have a special child, and then this guilt manifests as anger because I feel helpless. I prayed every night for my child. I was never angry with him; I often just felt helpless,' she said. 'For the last twelve years, I have denied that my son has ADHD. These labels are dangerous; they cause immense harm. The unfortunate thing with ADHD or any learning disorder is that the child is looked at as a symptom, as a problem. Do you know, my son is twelve years old and is a chatterbox, but he doesn't speak to his relatives? He goes and picks up conversations with strangers, with people who visit the house to do repairs and with the milkman. He knows that he is not judged by them; children know that we are judging them constantly.'

But that's what education did; one of the purposes that assessments and formal schooling fulfilled was to judge the abilities of such children to function in mainstream society. To go to school meant to be evaluated constantly, for every move made and every test written. But for most children like Vidyut and their mothers, there was judgement at home as well, from the father.

'When Vidyut was four, I was almost six months pregnant with my second child, and my husband was hell-bent on teaching Vidyut how to cycle. But my son could not even pedal. After trying multiple times to get him to balance, my husband gave up and started yelling at me. He just gave up,' she laughed out loud.

And just like figuring out what went wrong with Vidyut urinating in class, she had to figure this out as well. Her husband had judged her as incompetent and his child as 'not normal'. Heavily pregnant, she bent down as her son sat on the cycle, now with side wheels, to ensure there was balance. She realized her son was just resting his feet on the pedal, not pressing them. Her husband had kept yelling at him to put pressure on the pedal, but Vidyut didn't know what pressure meant.

'How is a four-year-old child, who couldn't even read at that time, supposed to know what pressure is?' Gayathri said with humour. For a few days, Gayathri bent down and pressed on the pedal with her hand as he sat. And soon enough, he learnt to cycle.

'When your child is good and achieves what society expects them to achieve, both parents take credit. But if the child does something wrong or is incapable of doing something, the blame is on the mother. The whole load of parenting is shifted to the woman, who has to figure out what's wrong,' she sighed.

Even though the blame for how a child behaves is routinely put on the mother, Gayathri and Vaishnavi have had to go above and beyond to prove themselves, not just as good mothers to their partners and their social circles but to themselves too. No one, perhaps not even the husbands, questioned whether it was only the mother's responsibility to educate the child. The expectation and belief that the mother is the primary caregiver wreaked havoc on what mothers wanted to do for themselves. Behind these stories of their children's success lay a different kind of education, one of discarding their certificates and qualifications and of learning anew every day *with* their child. Both child and mother were students again.

Here, it was not ADHD that was the problem, but rather that it brought to the fore inequalities of gendered notions of parenting and education. These notions indicated how and in what situations socially constructed knowledge could control behaviour and regulate thoughts and feelings.

But there was more. The child was not just the parents' responsibility. The child spent a large part of the day in school or engaged in school activities. The child was being groomed to become a future citizen, one who would take part in society and democracy. At this juncture, it becomes essential to question what the motivations of a school are. At one level, the school is engaged in producing future citizens, human capital, so to speak, to improve their skills so that they can participate within a globalized job market and increase their citizenship potential. As such, a school has an interest in shaping the minds and bodies of children to function in a particular way, which is productive for all of society. On the other hand, was the child then being treated as a means to something else that politics and culture wanted?

But before all this, there remained a larger question. Is ADHD even real and, more importantly, who gets to decide what it is?

A child wanting to run around could be diagnosed as hyperactive, a child interrupting or speaking out of turn or 'talking back', a complaint lodged on me often, could be labelled impulsive. Poor attention could be diagnosed as a child being disconnected from the conversation. The examples listed here could apply to any child at any particular time, and the direct implications of this philosophical conundrum were felt by the mothers and the children.

'How is it that ADHD seems to be a recent phenomenon?' I asked a leading educator with decades of experience in this field over yet another Zoom call. I couldn't help but imagine how difficult it must have been for teachers and parents to educate children during the pandemic through online classes. Indian schools had one of the longest closures across the world, more than eighty-two weeks.[2]

'In India, we had this joint family system. When the parent got tired, the responsibility of the child would be passed on to a grandparent, and then maybe to an aunt or even an older cousin. Perhaps, it's just that parents are spending more time with children,' she guffawed.

There was some inherent logic to that. It was certainly observable that Indian families were breaking up into smaller nuclear families.

'Having been a teacher for over thirty years, I can tell you that kids were originally not like this; there has been a shift. But I don't know if you can ascribe it to ADHD or something else. Perhaps, it is the way in which children are being taught, or perhaps growing up with a screen. Some research suggests that it could be because of changes in diets. But today, out of any ten kids, seven of them will have some attention issues. It probably won't fall under the strict diagnostic guidelines of what ADHD is, but there would be some issue,' the educator said.

While the joint family system has been touted as a great and important aspect of Indian tradition and also as a site of education, little is spoken about the detrimental effects it has on children's self-esteem and agency, and in some cases on educational outcomes as well, especially on the girl child.

But what really was this issue? According to Zakhif (name changed), a reputed occupational therapist in Chennai, ADHD does not have clear physical symptoms till date. No neurological signs, blood tests or brain scan findings can verify if a child has ADHD. There are no known causes or established remedies.

'But see, there are real consequences. Children with severe ADHD may face ostracization from peers, and their academic performance could be poor, leading to low self-esteem. They could face punishment or discipline more often. Parents find that through medication, through a drug like Ritalin or Adderall, the child can focus and go to school. Some doctors suggest giving it only during the school day; they suggest not to give it on weekends.' Zakhif said.

School education is universal and compulsory. Therefore, children cannot be excluded from a schooling apparatus, but a hyperactive child, this inattentive, disruptive soul had to be 'dealt with', and this 'dealing with' was happening in urban centres through the use of psychostimulants and therapy.

'If parents want their child to be part of the mainstream, they are forced to do this. The other option is to pull the child out of a regular school and put them in a "special school". But I am not particularly in favour of that. Schools and parents need to be patient. Schools ensure that all their pupils pass; parents want to show off that their child is smart and capable,' the educator sighed.

Through all this, the child and the mother had to continuously negotiate, with themselves and others, to retain or establish their 'normality'. They had to scan themselves and others, continuously adopting an evaluative gaze of what is normal and what is not. From my conversations with these mothers, I understood that this continuous negotiation and evaluation was exhausting.

'Of course, ADHD is real. It is a disorder, not a disease,' said Zakhif, when I met him at his spacious office and occupational therapy centre. He exuded enormous patience, something that felt highly necessary for what he was dealing with.

'But what matters more in India are the consequences of ADHD, not whether it exists. When I conduct an assessment and inform parents of the likelihood of their child having ADHD, lots of parents come to me and tell me, "I was also like this, sir." I ask them, was the environment the same? Was there so much sugar in our diets, so much saturated fats and preservatives? Did you spend so much time on your screens? Were there so many different kinds of radiation?' he said as if he were ranting.

He, too, was reiterating that the consequences of ADHD were what made it real.

'But I think the problem lies with educational institutions and the pressure that comes from them. We still have rules and laws that cater to a very small portion of the population. Only those few kids who will sit straight, obey the teacher, won't get distracted, won't look here and there will benefit from these rules. We as adults have enormous expectations from the child, but at the same time, we are unwilling to provide a nurturing environment. ADHD is very much real.'

Here was a qualified therapist, a practitioner with decades of experience and a whole gamut of qualifications choosing to put aside all the biomedical, biological and pathological connotations of ADHD and choosing to focus on what he actually thought it was—a disorder perpetuated by education systems and parenting.

Zakhif took on the role of a pragmatic and empathetic therapist. He was firm that in extreme cases, children had to be medicated. 'If the child has potential and you know the child can do better, these drugs should be given. It will help improve performance.' It was quite evident that improved performance through psychostimulants could have many positive ramifications. The child's self-esteem could go up, it could encourage more inclusion within the school set-up and, more importantly, parental acceptance and love could increase.

But medication for ADHD also has side effects such as possible growth suppression and the early onset of depression. The use of antidepressants has also been found to possibly increase the risk of suicide ideation.[3] In general, however, these risks are seen as worthwhile. Zakhif referred those children he thought required medication to psychiatrists, who would weigh the potential risks of medication against the benefits. In most cases, the medical treatment of ADHD was done through relatively 'safer' medical interventions, such as providing stimulants and/or inhibitors.

'Every year, there is a new problem we have to deal with. A few years ago, awareness was very low, so we had to spread awareness fast. The research is quite detailed and states that what happens between the ages of one and three leaves a lasting impression on the child's development. Now, the awareness is very high. Parents have Google and are part of multiple WhatsApp groups. So, they think they know everything,' Zakhif laughed. 'The way in which parents responded a decade or so ago is different from how they respond now. Now, they tell me how to treat the child.'

While Zakhif could only speak from his experience and was generalizing the patterns he observed, one would be loath to imagine that with greater awareness, things were getting better. 'There are therapy centres across the country which sugarcoat the diagnosis. Ninety per cent of parents are not able to accept the diagnosis that their child has some form of attention or learning disorder. So, they start arguing; they bring up experiences of what someone in their social circle is going through and correlate it with their child's experience. Then, they go to some other therapist or clinic, who will tell them what they want to hear,' he said as he looked out of the window. Clearly, a lot was running through his mind, the frustrations and the helplessness in seeing a child's development being squandered by parents.

'How long do you work with one child?' I asked, curious to understand more about the behaviour of parents. 'Five years ago, I would work with a child for two to three years and see wonderful results. Now, a child is able to stay for a maximum of six months,' he said.

'What do you mean "able to stay"?' I asked.

'They are not able to stick for long. People try alternative medicine or indulge in therapist shopping. Every few months, they move from one therapist to another. Parents are investing money; they want to see immediate results. They spend Rs 15,000 to 20,000 a month and are impatient to see that investment do something. But therapist shopping is really bad. It causes immense turmoil for a child; it takes time for a child with a learning or an attention disorder to get used to a place or a person,' he sighed.

From what Zakhif was saying, he was hinting at a different form of inclusion, one which required schools to function in a fundamentally different way. It also needed a rewiring of curricula, but more importantly, this new form of inclusion needed to come from parents.

'The funny thing, or actually the sad thing is,' Zakhif reflected, 'that in the ninety minutes I spend with a child in occupational therapy, I spend thirty minutes doing couples therapy. I tell the fathers to hold their wife's hands when they come home from work and ask her how she is doing. I have lost count of the number of times mothers have started crying when I have said that. It is a continuous blame game; the father says it is because of her; the mother says it is because of him. I have accepted that it is a part of my job to counsel couples also,' Zakhif laughed.

Within this entire spectrum, multiple people were competing for authority to determine the child's interest—parents, the state, therapists and doctors. They all could legitimately claim the authority to determine what defines well-being. But was the child a vehicle of interest for the parents and the state, or was the child a human being like the rest of us?

Certainly, one could argue that the creation of a body that is compliant is required for full participation in society. But from these conversations I had, one thing became clear: There seemed to be a lack of distinction between whether these psychostimulants helped increase academic performance or if they helped the child calm down and appear more 'normal'. But to be normal was to conform to a standard of statistically average behaviour.

There is a slippery slope in defining who is medically impaired and who merely is normal. This could raise further issues; the poor who would require medical intervention possibly have restricted access, while the rich may have more opportunity for mere enhancement. This could only lead to greater disparity in educational attainment.

ADHD remains a great philosophical problem for education. Can we claim ADHD to be a real phenomenon? If yes, on what basis, especially if there are no established causes, diagnosis and treatment? If a person were to be diagnosed with ADHD, do they have free will? Could you hold a child or an adult with ADHD morally responsible for their actions? And if they were to commit a crime, should they be punished? Within all of these questions lay a deeper problem of how to determine truth. But within the gamut of opinions and aspirations lay the day-to-day life of a child and the trials and tribulations of a mother. Through all these stories, there is a clear indication that the needs of the child have been married with the needs of the parents, the school and the state.

'Ever since childhood, I was told that I have to achieve something "special", be special to someone, do something special for someone. But as my son grew up, the word "special" took a very different turn for me,' Gayathri said, just as I was about to leave. 'The word "special" lost its significance. I started hating it, especially when my son was called a special child. Everyone has some problem or the other; we all behave erratically and impulsively many times. Does that mean I am special as well? I live for the word "normal".'

Chapter 6

Performance of Culture

'The power to impose the principles of the construction of reality—in particular, social reality—is seen as a major dimension of political power.'

—Pierre Bourdieu[1]

Srinath (name changed) took to the stage early in life, probably when he was eight or nine. An active debater, fervent orator and popular kid in school, he often represented his school in various oratorical and debating events. Srinath was born and raised in a Brahmin-dominated area in Chennai and went to a school with an overwhelming concentration of Brahmin students. Almost 99 per cent of the students came from Brahmin families of varying classes. Nearly all the teachers and staff were Brahmins, and the school proudly accepted and asserted its Brahmin identity. But this school wasn't an anomaly in Chennai. In fact, many of Chennai's elite private CBSE schools were Brahmin-dominated. It was as if they were a clique of their own, existing within their small world, steadfastly focused on their ideas of merit and success.

These schools were academically focused and some were hell-bent on the singular 'great Indian ambition' of getting their students to crack the competitive IIT-JEE. Besides that, they were also quite keen to organize large extracurricular fests. These fests, colloquially known as 'culturals', were multi-day festivals consisting of different competitions, where students from different schools could display their talents for prizes and bring glory to the school they were representing. Imagine the Triwizard tournament in the Harry Potter series but less fatal.

The competitions were wide-ranging. Schoolchildren would assemble bands to perform in music competitions, choreograph different types of dances, participate in art competitions and a range of thespian and literary competitions. Schools would host these 'culturals' for two to three days, and winners of each event would accrue points for their school. At the end of the festival, the school with the highest number of points would be crowned the winner. These culturals were extravagant affairs. Schools competed with each other not just through these competitions, but also on the scale at which they could organize such a fest. Celebrities were often chief guests, grounds of the school would be rented for food stalls from top restaurants in the city, the school would be decked up in large banners, and there generally was a very festive atmosphere. For many high school students, especially those not academically inclined, these culturals were the pinnacle of achievement. Some students were so good that they could single-handedly win five or six competitions and guarantee their school a victory in a particular festival. One such person was Srinath.

There must have been a few hundred people in that audience that day and plenty of young women Srinath was keen to impress. The auditorium was big and imposing, complete with roving spotlights, but more so was the stage. It was so huge that Srinath and his friends could have easily played a game of three-on-three football on it. The crowd was full of energy, screaming and cheering, for participants were competing for school pride, which was a big deal. You wanted to win the competition so that your school could win and you could be the hero, and perhaps that beautiful young woman you had a crush on would be impressed.

'Next up, we have Srinaaaatthhhhhhh . . .' announced the host, as if he were announcing the entry of Mike Tyson or Muhammad Ali. Srinath jumped on the stage, mic in hand, to hear hundreds of people cheering and hooting for him. He was a popular figure in the culturals' circuit, having spun his charm and magic in multiple events over the last year.

This particular event he was participating in was known as 'shipwreck'. It was an improvisational literary event where each participant would be given a famous character to impersonate and had to convince the judges why they should be given the last life jacket on a sinking ship. The criteria for winning primarily involved humour and an ability to impress the crowd but also thinking on your feet, making logical arguments and not stuttering or stammering while on stage. The kind of characters picked for this competition ranged from famous politicians, both local and international, to pop icons, including Michael Jackson, Cardi B and film stars, apart from whatever the judge felt like on that particular day. So, for example, if you were given the character of Manmohan Singh, you had to impersonate him and convince the judges (and the audience) why you deserved the last life jacket on the sinking ship.

Srinath walked on stage, chest out as if he were a boxer entering the ring, with all the confidence in the world. The character given to him was Kanye West, a popular American rapper, singer and songwriter. Like all other participants, Srinath was given only three minutes to prepare. The spotlight was on him, an adoring crowd of hundreds would listen to his every word, waiting to burst out laughing at the slightest hint of something funny. For the next eight minutes, Srinath tried to convince the audience how giving him the last life jacket would ensure that Kanye West could run for the presidency in

America and that he would ensure the show 'Keeping Up with the Kardashians' would be stopped. The audience laughed out loud, and the judges looked impressed, even as Srinath ended his eight minutes by telling the judge that he would tag him on social media and ensure that he got a million followers in a day.

'To be successful in these events, you had to play to the judges, and you had to play to how they responded. You had to be quick on your feet and creatively connect to people's knowledge and perceptions of that character. You need to know a lot about pop culture. You need to be able to rebut challenging questions and be very emphatic in your statements,' Srinath said when I asked him what it took to be successful at these events.

Students from other schools came and performed, each got eight minutes; one got the character of Ravi Shastri, another got the character of Rahul Gandhi, and one even got the character of Poonam Pandey, a famous adult star in India. The reactions varied; some students couldn't elicit any response from the audience, while others did. Meanwhile, multiple other competitions were happening at other venues in the school.

Ashwath (name changed) sat eagerly with his two teammates, pen and paper in hand, waiting for the quiz to start. The quiz was another marquee event in the culturals, an event for people to display how much they knew. For people like Ashwath, it offered a space to express and compete, away from the hyper-expecting crowd of performative literary events. Ashwath claimed that he couldn't sing to save his life, dance never appealed to him and the most he could draw was a crooked stick figure. Getting on stage and competing with Srinath was too tall a task, and in any case, Ashwath felt more at home while quizzing. He found that he could connect the dots well and quizzing gave him an excellent platform to succeed. More importantly, he wanted to win something for his school and have his schoolmates give him the kind of adulation that they gave Srinath.

'A good quiz is when an answer is known to a large majority. Most of the quizzes in these culturals don't test your ability to remember. They won't ask how tall Everest is; they expect you to connect the dots,' Ashwath said.

'The more quizzes you went for, the more you became accustomed to the pattern of questions and how to connect the dots. You kind of develop an intuition about what to connect,' he continued.

It also helped that Chennai had a very active quizzing scene dominated by the alumni of the elite Brahminical schools. Until 2015, Chennai played host to some of the most significant quizzes in India, including the Landmark quiz, which took place every year to a packed audience of more than 1500 at Chennai's famed Music Academy auditorium. An organization to propagate quizzing culture, called the Quiz Foundation of India, met regularly on weekends. In an education system dominated by a need to perform knowledge continuously, quizzes provided an active forum to do so.

'I always felt that these literary events like shipwreck were never aspirational for me; it was easy to accept that I was better at something else. The culturals team clearly told me that I was here to quiz and get those points. I had a specific role, and I was to fulfil it to the best of my ability. Most schools would have had a half-empty or an empty auditorium when a quiz was happening. When a shipwreck was happening, it would be full,' Ashwath sighed. He, too, wanted the adulation that Srinath regularly received.

Soon enough, the quiz master started the quiz, and Ashwath and the gang got down to cracking the questions. A set of thirty questions formed the preliminary round, which they topped easily—cracking twenty-four of the thirty. The finals would be an on-stage affair the next day, hopefully in front of a packed auditorium.

In Ashwath's words, success in these quizzes required a lot of 'exposure', a term that captured the social and cultural capital[2] that students from these schools grew up with. Capital no longer means physical, transferable, tangible resources such as money, land, machinery or buildings. Capital today could involve intangible, non-physical forms, such as social networks, and access to and possession of knowledge and skills, certificates and diplomas amongst many others. Exposure meant access to different forms of capital, something that students of oppressed castes didn't have access to and something easily available for students like Ashwath.

A quiz, a shipwreck, an arts-based competition, or a dance competition usually happened simultaneously during these culturals. The audience was generally comprised of students from the host school and students from other schools who had come to participate. The host school was not allowed to participate in the fest it organized. They were expected to fill the auditoriums and the classrooms where these competitions would happen to give it a big-event feel. Very few saw it as an opportunity to learn and understand; for most, it was an opportunity to get away from a few hours of class.

Meanwhile, the results were out; Srinath had won the shipwreck competition by an overwhelming margin. He was the first to get points for his school in the overall points table. A first place in shipwreck, a second place in battle of the bands, and two third places in art-based events ensured that Srinath's school was on top, with many of his peers also having qualified from the preliminaries to the final rounds of other competitions. But Srinath had achieved something special. His first-place victory in shipwreck allowed him to enter the winner's event, the traditional finale of all culturals in these Chennai schools. The winner's event consisted of a series of competitions for which the winners of different literary or thespian events qualified automatically. In this event, they had to participate in a series of competitions, which included being given sixty seconds to showcase their talents, an anti-shipwreck, where the rules of a traditional shipwreck were twisted, and they had to convince the judges why that celebrity they were impersonating should not be given the life jacket; sometimes, there would also be a debate or even a small quiz. Most of the events were oratorical and relied on the judges' discretion. It often happened in front of huge audiences. People who qualified for the winner's event could often have their way with their school headmaster and bring in many of their classmates and friends for support. The winner's event winner was usually awarded twice the number of points that winning a regular competition would have gotten them. Hence, it was a huge deal.

Raghavan (name changed) tapped his feet nervously; he was to go up against Srinath in another literary event named block and tackle, and his school's points were very close to that of Srinath's school on the overall points board. He did not have the popular support that Srinath had though he knew he was better than Srinath in this event. Block and tackle required an exceptional ability to think on your feet. It was a competition where the participant would be given two sides of the same debate and had to speak for and against the topic. When the judge said 'block', you had to speak for the topic, and when the judge said 'tackle', you had to speak against it, and often the judge would change their mind in a matter of seconds. Raghavan was given the topic 'Messi vs Ronaldo: Who is the greatest footballer?' When the judge would say 'block,' Raghavan had to speak in support of Messi, and when the judge would say 'tackle', he had to speak in support of Ronaldo. Being given just three minutes to prepare, Raghavan decided to wing it. After all, this was a topic of great passion for him, and he could narrate statistics about these footballers even in his sleep. 'Next up, we have Raghavan,' said the host from far away. There was hardly anybody to cheer, and in the middle of a hot Chennai day, the few present were busy fanning themselves and making plans to get something to eat. Slightly dejected, Raghavan got on stage.

'Are you ready?' the judge asked.

Raghavan gulped and nodded.

'Block,' announced the judge, and Raghavan shot off.

'Messi is the greatest footballer in the world; just look at the number of goals he has scored and how he can change the game just by his presence. He is also one of the most loyal footballers and has been at the same club since the age of sixteen. Ronaldo shifted four clubs in his career, but Messi has stayed in just one, and that shows that to be a great footballer, you need to be a loyal one as well,' said Raghavan at breakneck speed.

'Tackle,' announced the judge suddenly, and Raghavan had to change his stance.

'But you see, Ronaldo has shown that while anyone with talent can play, it takes a lot of grit to come out of absolute poverty and do what he has done. Sure, you can play in one club all your life, but to go from country to country and club to club and achieve success everywhere is something unique. It's like Srinath versus me, he is naturally talented, but I worked hard on my English to come to perform here. So, whom would you rather support?' Raghavan's tongue-in-cheek comment elicited chuckles from the sparse audience and a loud laugh from the judge. Srinath sat stone-faced in the corner, unhappy about the subtle jibe.

'Block,' said the judge again.

'Messi has won more Ballon d'Or's than Ronaldo; it just shows that he is substantially better than Ronaldo . . .' Raghavan continued his spiel. Finally, at the end of what seemed like a speedy six minutes, the judge said he was done and began scribbling scores and possibly feedback on an A4 sheet. The judging criteria were never uniform and varied from judge to judge, so it was hard to predict.

Srinath started giving himself a pep talk. 'You are the best, and you know it,' he said, slapping himself on the cheek as if riling himself up for a boxing match. 'Next up, we have Srinath,' said the host, rather dispiritedly. But it didn't bother Srinath; his earlier exploits in shipwreck had given him enough adulation, making him willing to overlook the loss of attention in this one. The topic given to him was 'Betty vs Veronica: Who deserves Archie more?'. Srinath looked back at the judge, flabbergasted. He had no idea about Betty, Veronica or Archie. He had never read an Archie comic book before.

'But, sir, I don't know anything about this topic . . .' he stammered, his confidence evaporating as beads of sweat glistened on his forehead. The judge maintained that there was nothing he could do to change the topic and that he would give him a few extra minutes to prepare, and he could use his phone and look it up online if he wanted. Fuming at this injustice, Srinath took out his phone and searched for articles on this debate. It didn't make any sense to him. He read as fast as he could, but his legs started shaking, and he could feel his shirt becoming sweatier and sweatier. 'Block,' said the judge, suddenly signalling that his time was up, and Srinath hastily put his phone back in his pocket.

'Betty is a poor girl, so she deserves Archie more,' he stammered and stood, not knowing what else to say.

The judge waited, seeing if there was something more Srinath had to say. A few agonizing moments later, the judge announced, 'Tackle'.

'Veronica has more money and can obviously keep Archie happier,' he said, staying quiet again.

This time Srinath's anger was evident. After ages, the judge sighed and said his time was up.

Srinath got off the stage, red-faced. He had never felt this humiliated before. The judge had intentionally screwed him over, which was not a new phenomenon. The judges in these culturals were previous winners of these events and almost always alumni of the close-knit set of elite private schools in Chennai. They were mostly young college students or people who had just finished college.

'I have been invited to judge so many shipwrecks and block and tackles after I finished school,' recollected Srinath fondly. Depending on the school and students' influence, a celebrity would occasionally come as a judge. In the eyes of the teachers and principals, these celebrities—mostly actors from the Tamil film industry—never made for good judges. English was the de facto language, and speaking Tamil was looked down upon. These celebrities never bothered speaking in English much. 'Beyond a point, the same judges came in different combinations, so if you had made a good impression earlier, winning became a whole lot easier,' Raghavan recollected.

This phenomenon of these judges being contemporaries of each other, just a few years older but having achieved fame within this small, close-knit community of Brahminical schools, created a nepotistic structure that favoured those who were part of the 'in' crowd. Those who knew the judges beforehand and had made a good impression stood a much greater chance of winning. Disappointing scores of some groups (and the success of others) in culturals was not really always because of the differences in skill that participants had but more a consequence of how these schools operated and organized these events. If you had the appropriate cultural capital and were in the good books of the judges, you would be successful.

Here, cultural capital was a consequence of caste and class. Out of all these schools that participated in culturals in Chennai, there was rarely a school that catered to underprivileged students or even a school that followed a different curriculum, such as that of the Tamil Nadu State Board. It was a cluster of private CBSE schools that routinely participated in each other's culturals year after year, decade after decade. The students of these schools came from a particular class and caste background. In the system of culturals in private schools in Chennai, students and teachers recognized only those who were like them, in terms of caste, culture and social presence.

These culturals cemented the notion of a small world. They established a dominant discourse of conducting these events only in English, making international pop-culture references and calling the same judges repeatedly. Any reference to local pop culture and to indigenous art and craft were all looked down upon. If a student did the shipwreck in Tamil, they would be disqualified—it was considered inappropriate, as if it vilified the reputation of the school. 'People dancing to fast-paced Tamil film songs or singing popular songs that had lyrics deemed as inappropriate were immediately disqualified,' Srinath recollected. There was a code about what was appropriate and what was not, what would be accepted and what wouldn't. Most importantly, the authority to decide this lay in the hands of a few schools and its stakeholders, such as the administrators, teachers, students and their parents.

Those with the appropriate culture are reinforced with success, while others are not. In establishing the dominant discourse, the school, its teachers, students and their parents constructed their own reality and took offence when another reality was shown to them. Culturals, and these schools that actively took part in them, became involved in a battle to classify one another, that a particular set of schools and their students were 'better' in some way, that they could provide some advantages other schools couldn't. It became a method to maintain the social order of caste and class.[3] 'My son is so gifted' was a common refrain I remember hearing throughout my school days as well. This notion of 'giftedness', openly celebrated in these culturals, helps reinforce the idea that students who win these competitions do so completely based on their merit. I had asked Srinath, Ashwath and a few others if they ever had training for any of these events. All of them said that they hadn't. By making students perceive their achievements through these culturals as a natural ability, culturals constantly reinforce meritocracy as the natural order of things and that the world is a level playing field for everyone, that privilege doesn't matter. Srinath, Ashwath and all the other students of these schools were embodying their privilege on stage.

The prizes that students got for winning competitions were also a clear sign of privilege. In some of the more prominent elite schools' culturals, the winner of shipwrecks got DVD players, tablets, television sets and even mobile phones. Sometimes, there were gift vouchers of large denominations and almost always a trophy and a certificate.

Srinath sat alone, feeling humiliated. Meanwhile, the results of the block and tackle were announced. Raghavan had won first place and secured a place in the winner's event. The prize for winning the block and tackle event was an Amazon gift card worth Rs 5000. Srinath had won the same prize for winning shipwreck. Raghavan had a smug smile on his face. He was tired of coming second to Srinath in multiple competitions. He felt like he had settled a score. Srinath walked up to Raghavan. 'I will see you in the winner's event,' Srinath said. Jealousy and feelings of entitlement weren't particularly new concepts amongst high-school teenagers, but these cultural fests heightened them. There was a lot at stake. An Amazon gift voucher for Rs 5000 would be useful to anyone, even more so for a sixteen-year-old teenager. Moreover, Srinath couldn't get those points on the board for his school, while Raghavan had secured full points. Both schools were now neck to neck on the leaderboard.

In these events, judges had an outsized role. Their discretion often tilted fortunes and was a continuous subject of discussion. After each event, students would huddle together and discuss at length how good or bad the judge was. As much as popular students like Srinath or Raghavan were the centre of attention, these judges were too.

'How long have you been judging these events?' I asked a young college student over a Zoom call. He had been particularly successful in the fest circuit, especially in events like shipwreck and block and tackle and was called to judge regularly every year.

'Ever since I left school, they kept calling me back. Every school wants to maintain a standard for all the competitions, and judges make all the difference. It is difficult for a school to get someone new and expect them to run a particular event like block and tackle the way they want. Juniors from these schools knew that I had an excellent track record, and they knew that I knew how to judge,' he said thoughtfully. 'But you know, judging is not easy; you must also perform there. You have to be witty; you have to ensure the audience is entertained; you have to show you're still good.'

'What kept bringing you back to these culturals? Why did you still want to judge?' I asked.

'It's very personal to me. Culturals have been a catalyst in my life. It's because of these experiences that I can speak English to an extent. Until performing in these events, my English was terrible. After culturals, I have been a very different person. This is my way of giving back. But most importantly, they trusted me to do a good job,' he replied.

The element of trust certainly played a big role because these culturals were ultimately a performance. It showcased participants' talents, which they believed came to them naturally. It was an opportunity for the judges to flaunt their ability to maintain the 'standards' of a good event. For the school, it was an affirmation that they were not just bastions of rote learning but also organizers of engaging extracurricular activities where a level playing field was provided for all. However, what remained unsaid was that all these performances happened behind a translucent curtain. These schools perceived the playing field as level only because they could not recognize others. For example, a student performing Tamil hip-hop or rap, or a Tamil folk dance would have been disqualified for being inappropriate. In that sense, these schools didn't recognize anyone who wanted to do something different. For these schools and the students, their playing field constituted only themselves. In such a situation, performance in these culturals became a performance of their privilege.

But performance took on different roles and meanings, especially if you were a girl in these schools. Vidya (name changed) was a girl brimming with confidence and talent. Events like shipwreck and block and tackle were male-dominated events, while the girls mostly participated in dance and art competitions. In their own way, culturals reinforced gender hierarchies tacitly by choosing who could perform in what competitions. But Vidya was a girl who wanted to participate in literary events, and she did. In most culturals she participated in, she was the only girl in the block and tackle and shipwreck events. 'I felt judged more objectively because I was a girl. Judges were wary because they had to figure out how to explain why I lost. But also, the number of times I have lost in these competitions because I am a girl . . .' she scoffed angrily.

In 2015, Vidya won the winner's event defeating five boys—a feat unheard of till then. It probably hasn't yet been repeated. The fact that very few girls (in this case, just one) could achieve this kind of success spoke volumes about the structures and obstacles that worked to keep people like Vidya out.

'I was quite experienced in these events by the time I reached twelfth grade. I had gotten better because I had practice and exposure,' Vidya stated, recollecting a story of a block and tackle event she had taken part in that year. 'My topic was "Sambhar or Rasam", which was quite easy for me. I thought I did really well. But when the results were announced, a boy had won first place, and I was second. The judge was scared that if he had given the first prize to me, a girl, he'd have been accused of favouritism or perversion. I was quite upset, and then a teacher approached me and congratulated me on being the only girl in the event.'

* * *

The tension within the two schools Srinath and Raghavan represented had surged. Srinath was extremely sour at the treatment meted out to him in the block and tackle event; Raghavan maintained that he did whatever he could and performed well on the topic given to him. The winner's event was the next day, with both schools rooting for their respective participants. School pride was a big deal.

The winner's event is a spectacle. Schools often book out the most sought-after performance auditoriums in the city— some with more than a thousand seats and ensure it's filled up. There is great buzz and hype around the event and the judges. The bigger and more prestigious schools go out of their way to ensure the grandiosity of this event by getting in big sponsors and calling celebrity guests and judges. But the spotlight is on those who qualified for the winner's event. Schools work hard to outdo each other for the winner's event prizes. Some schools give mobile phones, some flat-screen TVs, and some even laptops. Srinath joked that he knew of a senior from school who had won so many of these gadgets that he could now set up an electronics retail store.

The auditorium was packed, with the stage decorated in the school's colours and a huge banner printed with the words 'WINNER'S EVENT'. A DJ was present by the stage, playing the latest English and Tamil hits, keeping the audience's mood upbeat. There was a buzz in the air, with students of Srinath's and Raghavan's schools coming in droves to provide support. One could spot plenty of young couples holding hands, for it was one of the rare occasions where all the teachers were busy getting the event up and running and wouldn't have time to moral police the students.

The participants of the winner's event got on stage one by one to the announcement of their names, which could barely be heard owing to the loud cheers that each student got. In total, this event had six participants. All of these participants had won literary/oratory events that emphasized proficiency in English. It was as if people who were good at music, dance or art and had won in those events weren't good enough to be winners.

The stakes were high for Srinath and Raghavan; the winner of this event would ensure that their school won the overall fest. Moreover, the winner of this event would walk home with a brand-new Apple laptop. Srinath, Raghavan and other participants enthralled the audience. They spoke with passion, they joked, they imitated personalities, and they even danced. There could be only one winner, though, most likely male. Having brought glory to their school, they would walk home with an Apple laptop.

Culturals created a talent hierarchy, instilling the belief that whoever won did so because they were a lot more talented than others. Perhaps they were, but this process also blinded everyone who took part in the roles their particular school played. It made inequality seem natural and even justified. The skills of oratory, style, taste, wit and command over the English language, which appeared natural for the Brahmin classes, were skills that students of other backgrounds had to strive for. Students from less privileged backgrounds could only acquire with great effort what appeared to come naturally to these dominant caste students. As a result, these culturals almost always saw dominant-caste, upper-class students, usually boys, performing at and winning these events.

This system naturalized the culture of Brahmins as appropriate, as how things should be. The less privileged (read oppressed-caste students) had no choice but to labour to imitate what appeared to come naturally to the successful people in culturals because of the notions of what is appropriate or not was defined by these Brahminical schools.[4]

Through researching and writing this chapter, I began to understand that there are multiple ways in which we perceive success and that particular groups hold power in defining what success is and how it is perceived. In such a scenario, these culturals contribute to a situation where the elite schools can now claim cultural performativity as proof of their merit, leading to networks of caste solidarity, further exacerbating caste divides and inequities.

One day, Vidya was representing her school in an English oratorical competition organized by an NGO. It was held in a small hall with students from various schools—not just the elite CBSE ones. It was Vidya's turn, and she went up on stage and, as always, performed naturally and well. 'After I got off stage, one boy came up to me. He was wearing the uniform of one of the state board schools. He said, "Akka, you should win. English *superaa pesringa* (you are speaking English really well)",' she recollected. The boy's rationale was that Vidya deserved to win because she could speak English really well and effortlessly. The 'us' versus 'them' divide was made clear through particular performances, especially ones that required students to speak good English. This disparity was created by the schools themselves, maybe not by intention but certainly by design. In that sense, the divide becomes something of a natural entity, something that just 'is'. It is a consequence of educational processes.

Chapter 7

Teaching History the 'Right' Way

'As a classroom community, our capacity to generate excitement is deeply affected by our interest in one another, in hearing one another's voices, in recognizing one another's presence.'

—bell hooks[1]

'The educator has the duty of not being neutral.'

—Paulo Freire[2]

For six years between 2013 and 2019, I was an educator and an entrepreneur, having launched an education start-up in Chennai to offer workshops in public speaking and debate to elementary and high school children. These were a very engaging and creative few years. Through public speaking and debate, we were attempting to get students to engage with history, philosophy and economics and had taught more than 5000 students across South India. I would be in different private schools through the week, taking classes and tailoring our courses and modules to the needs of the schools. Slowly but surely, we gained some reputation within a bunch of elite private schools.

'We want you to help us rewrite the history curriculum for Classes 6, 7 and 8. These textbooks are not enough,' said the director of a school, a prominent one, that had a reputation for academic excellence. The director was young and tall, clean-shaven, with trimmed hair—his face emanating the energy of a young schoolboy. He wore gold-rimmed spectacles, a crisp white formal shirt and grey pants and would not have been older than thirty-five, relatively young to handle an entire private school network. I had tried pitching our courses to this school for a couple of years, but this history curriculum idea was unexpected.

I sat, processing the statement and what he was asking of me.

'We need a fresh pair of eyes, a youngster's take to make history less boring,' he told me with a disarming smile, while the much older school correspondent looked on, amused by this conversation.

The room we sat in resembled a typical school administrator's room in a private school. It had a neat desk, a buzzer that would summon an attendant and a large portrait of the school's founder. Trophies and awards that the school had won were showcased strategically. These rooms always appeared straightforward, unlike the conversation he was trying to have with me.

I looked back at the director and correspondent, unsure. While I had experience teaching and creating curriculum and lesson plans for social science, I wondered if I could do it within a rigid school setting. The director rang the buzzer and called for some tea.

'Sir, it's a great honour, but I am not sure what you expect of me here,' I said.

'It's simple,' he said, fishing out the history textbooks of Classes 6, 7 and 8 from his desk drawer 'We will identify three chapters we can remove in each grade, and you will write three chapters to replace them.'

My eyes lit up.

'You want me to write a textbook for your school?' I asked, my voice barely able to conceal my excitement.

I mumbled excitedly about how so much of our history has been overlooked. I said I wanted to write about history that was contemporary and relevant to students so that they could make sense of the world today. I suppose my interest in history came from my days of participating in debate tournaments in college, where I learnt about historical events that had a direct impact on my life today. I was able to make more sense of my world as a result of what I learnt. I felt that history hadn't been properly taught to me in school. My history teacher was all about the details, the years, the dates and the names. My school was all about grades and performance; it was about getting into IITs, and history barely mattered. But I loved history, and I wanted students to love it as well. I had created a curriculum for the students I taught through my start-up and helped them look beyond science and math and think about the world.

'Your tea,' the director pointed to the untouched, now cold cup of tea in front of me as I rattled on, barely pausing to take a breath. In that instant, I thought they were just humouring me. I remember the director and the correspondent had a smile on their faces; but they looked satisfied and asked me when I could start. I was to start work in three days. I was twenty-four when I was given this assignment. In retrospect, it seems like a crazy idea for the director to have engaged with someone so young. But I was young and spirited, and I distinctly remember feeling that I could change the world, and the textbook was the first stepping stone to achieve that goal.

Classrooms are spaces where teachers and students make meaning, and in that sense, it is a dynamic space. It is not a neutral environment, and one classroom cannot be spoken of in the same way as another. While classrooms are an important space for the dissemination of the duties of the school, textbooks play a key role as well. The classroom, the textbook and the teacher form an important and indispensable triad in school-based education.

A lot of attention is given to the teacher, on their qualities and qualifications, and some attention to the design of the classroom, but the textbook and its content are taken as an indispensable truth. The textbook can exist neutrally, as an object uninfluenced by what happens inside the classroom, and it often does.

I was used to standing in front of a classroom as a teacher or as a student in a classroom doodling away at my desk. Being called to rewrite a textbook was something I had not imagined, and I was very excited.

On my first day, I strode in, full of excitement. I was directed to a desk that had been arranged for me in the administrative office. I waited for the director to report to work and introduce me to the principal and teachers. I later learnt that they had no idea who I was or what I had been appointed for. I got to work and typed out a rough work plan for the next two months, detailing my deliverables and each chapter's contents.

'Sir won't come in any time soon,' said a woman sitting behind a computer screen. She must have noticed my fidgeting, waiting for almost two hours for the director to arrive. I continued fiddling with my phone and tapping my feet loudly when the door opened and the director strode in.

'Let's meet in my room,' he announced and walked away, and I hurriedly put my phone in my pocket and followed him with my laptop.

'When you are in school, you are expected to keep your phone away. And from tomorrow, please come to school in formal attire,' he said, sizing me up. I was dressed in a long lavender kurta and jeans, an attire I had fashioned for myself as a teacher. I stood silently, a little taken aback. 'In this school, we emphasize decorum, and as a young consultant, you are also expected to follow it. Am I making myself clear?' he asked.

Being told off was not new to me. Being scolded had been an innate part of my experience, but that was with friends and family and lovers. Being scolded by an adult male who was not my father or teacher but someone who had hired me for a job was unsettling. I couldn't understand it, but I was also so taken with the idea of being given this opportunity that I felt that I deserved this patronizing tone.

'Yes, sir,' I gulped, looking back at him with surprise.

'Now, let's get to work,' he signalled to me to take a seat.

'Sir, here's a tentative plan I have made,' I began.

I narrated to him my plan for the textbooks. We could remove three chapters for each class depending on what the teachers found hard to teach and what the students found less interesting. He looked back at me emotionlessly.

'Sir, for the three replacement chapters for each class, I thought we could divide it over two broad themes—the history of India after Independence and the history of World War I and World War II,' I explained, regaining my enthusiasm. Again, he looked back at me with that same expressionless face.

'It is important we match ideologically here. I don't want these textbooks to teach our students something we don't want them to learn. It has to be objective and factual,' he said, with an emphasis on 'objective'. I should have understood then that, as in many places in the world, people's versions of history differ. The past is always a battleground, but for some reason, I earnestly held the hope that it could be overcome.

'Sir, there has been a lot written about both these themes; there is plenty of great video content. Real events have happened, and I was just thinking of narrating these events as stories and allowing for discussion with the teacher,' I said with confidence.

'Give me a couple of sample chapters, and we will take it from there,' he said, signalling the end of the conversation.

I had my task cut out. I was to interview the school principal and understand how the school approached its day-to-day academics. I was to interview teachers, profile them, and write the textbook accordingly, and I was also to sit in on classes and understand the behaviour of students.

One teacher I interacted with was Mrs Manimegalai (name changed). She had been teaching social science at the school for over twenty years. 'As a teacher within a school set-up, our priority is to finish the syllabus,' she said. She taught social science to Classes 6, 7 and 8 and warmly welcomed me to sit in on her classes.

I took a seat on the last bench, sharing it with three other seventh-grade boys, who looked like they had just discovered a treasure chest.

'Sir, welcome to the last bench. My name is Trishul,' said the boy sitting right next to me. He extended his hand, unable for some reason to conceal his excitement.

'Attention, everyone,' came the shrill voice of Mrs Manimegalai, and everyone sat upright and focused on her. 'Karthik, stand up and start reading Chapter 6. We are starting a new chapter today; this chapter will be a part of next week's test,' she said.

Everyone silently looked back at her, including me. Karthik began reading, while everyone was expected to follow what he was reading with their fingers on the textbook. The slightest infraction or disturbance was dealt with strictly. Soon enough, Trishul and the boy next to him were sent out of class for playing a game of 'book cricket'.[3] I continued sitting, taking notes and observing the class while they were made to stand outside. I could feel the disapproving gaze of the teacher on me as if I had instigated them to start playing that game in class.

I had gone through a similar pedagogy when I was in school. My history teacher made different students stand up and read a particular section of the textbook. In tandem, everyone read along silently, or at least they pretended to. I remember I was always particularly enthused when I was given a chance to read.

But this form of pedagogy was neither engaging nor instructive. Instead, it served to mechanically fulfil what Mrs Manimegalai said was a priority—completing the syllabus.

After completing a few more interviews with teachers who aired similar opinions and sitting in similarly tepid classes, I decided to get to work. I wanted to write these chapters in a way that engaged the student when they were reading and also wanted to assign activities in which they could apply what they read.

I got back to my desk in the administrative office and began writing. I was keen to work on the history of India post-Independence. This subject was slated for Classes 11 and 12 in the NCERT syllabus, but with many students opting to study science, I figured it would be interesting and relevant for them to study it now, to study a more contemporary history and something that affected processes and culture around them. However, the fact that this content was completely in the hands of teachers, of whom many were uninterested in making things interactive, weighed heavily on me. The priority, as unanimously stated by all the teachers I interviewed, was to complete the syllabus so that students could write the exams. What was learnt and how much of it was learnt, was not the point.

The cooperation of teachers in the school was difficult to obtain. I was, at best, a hindrance. These were teachers with decades of experience and I could gauge their thoughts by the way they looked at me. 'Who is this young boy trying to tell me how to teach social science? I have been doing it for decades.' I decided to reach out to other social science teachers in other schools, cities and states to get a bigger perspective.

'In school, I had great teachers and that was because I was in a very good school,' said Rajan, as we settled down for a chat. Rajan (name changed) was a unique teacher; he had obtained a master's in history and a PhD in archaeology and had been a teacher in a government school in North Delhi. It was not common in India for schoolteachers to have PhDs. He later taught at a private school in Pune before teaching at an international school in Bangalore. 'My teacher taught history not from one perspective but taught us empathy through history. If you look at Akbar's reign, you will find that two people have left accounts of that time. Abul Fazl has written favourably about Akbar, while Badayuni was critical. My teacher taught us to look at the historian first before reading the history. She didn't teach from the textbook. In our time, textbooks were pretty much showpieces,' he said. 'At the end of the day, textbooks should be used as a reference. The onus falls on the teacher and the school about how to teach the content. In my case, textbooks didn't do me much good.'

In a country where almost 60 per cent of students in Class 5 cannot read a Class 2 text, writing a textbook just for reference appears far-fetched. 'You would be surprised to see the work social science teachers are expected to do. In my school in Pune, they couldn't find a social science teacher, so they hired an English teacher to teach social science. Social science was seen as a method to teach English.'

Rajan paused and then added, 'It really depends on what your aim of teaching social science is. For most schools, it is about teaching literacy. If kids cannot read, what is the use of textbooks?'

Back at school where I was tasked to write new chapters, I wrote the first one titled 'A Divided India'. It was based on the events that happened just before 15 August 1947 and immediately after. History textbooks until Class 10 seemed to have a hard stop on a particular date—15 August 1947. It was as if history didn't exist beyond that point. My chapter included a section on Cyril Radcliffe, after whom the Radcliffe Line (the international border between India and Pakistan) is named and how he drew the line to separate the country 'between two people fanatically at odds with their different diets and incompatible gods, with the maps at disposal out of date and the Census Returns almost certainly incorrect'.[4] It also had detailed descriptions of the Hindu–Muslim riots right before Independence. The chapter ended with a quote from former prime minister Manmohan Singh: 'I dream of a day, while retaining our respective national identities, one can have breakfast in Amritsar, lunch in Lahore and dinner in Kabul. That is how my forefathers lived. That is how I want our grandchildren to live.'[5]

The next chapter, titled 'An Integrated India', focused on Sardar Vallabhbhai Patel's approach to reintegrating the princely states. It also included snippets of erstwhile princely states or kingdoms, such as Junagadh, Manipur and Hyderabad, which were integrated into the Indian union after some friction. Both the chapters included detailed performative exercises to help students retain the material. The exercises included making a speech as Jawaharlal Nehru asking Hindus and Muslims to stop the communal violence in 1947 and writing a letter as Sardar Vallabhbhai Patel to a ruler of a princely state asking them to accede to the Indian union. Writing this was a heady experience. I was certain that this was a radical, never-seen-before approach to history in Chennai schools.

The administrative office where I worked was noisy for two reasons: the continuous stream of visitors that an administrative office of a large private school gets and the chatty staff. The office being a largely unconducive atmosphere to write in, I wrote to the director seeking his permission to write from home while I stuck to the mutually agreed plan regarding deliverables. He agreed, and I continued my work from home. Soon enough, I sent in the first two chapters for him to view and share feedback on. After several days, I got a terse reply from him. 'I haven't seen you in school for a while. Please report immediately.'

Perturbed, I went back to school the next day, taking extra care to iron my shirt minutes before I left to ensure I was maintaining 'decorum'.

'Please sit,' he beckoned as I walked into his office. The expression on his face was as blank as the colour of the walls in his office. 'What had we agreed upon when we first discussed this project?' he started.

I stared, perplexed and at a loss for words. 'I am not sure what you are talking about, Sir.'

He turned his screen towards me to reveal my chapter; large parts were highlighted in red. 'We had agreed you would be objective and factual,' he said, with a stern look in his eyes. 'Look,' he pointed. 'You have mentioned Mohammed Ali Jinnah; you have mentioned that Hindus, Muslims and Sikhs lived in relative harmony. You have mentioned Manmohan Singh and some dream of his wanting to go to Pakistan; why have you mentioned Nehru so many times?' he continued furiously and turned the screen away from me.

I stared back, taking a while to process what he had just said. This was a chartered accountant and an IIM Ahmedabad graduate getting furious at my mention of Jawaharlal Nehru and Manmohan Singh, former prime ministers of India.

'But sir . . .' I sputtered. 'I believe if we want to talk about the history of India just before and after Independence, it is obviously important to talk about Nehru and the Partition.'

'You may be ideologically inclined in some other way; that is not my business. But when you are in my school and writing for my students, I expect you to teach them the correct history. Am I making myself clear?' he asked, with the slightest hint of his voice escalating.

What was 'correct history'? It was now clear where he was coming from and what I had unwittingly gotten myself into. I was asked to write a history textbook from a 'neutral' standpoint, making the content closed to interpretations and offering only the 'official' history. As a novice, I hadn't read between the lines. I only saw the opportunity in front of me—to write a textbook

and, in my head, to start changing the world. I should have known
a lot earlier.

* * *

Textbooks have always been a site of political contestation in
India, and they remain so to this day. Before 1961, most social
science textbooks, particularly history, carried colonial stereotypes
coupled with communal prejudices. Romila Thapar, an acclaimed
historian and a scholar, was asked by UNESCO to review a series
of social science textbooks in Delhi. She noted that she was
' . . . appalled by the quality of the information that was being
conveyed in these books, with an adherence to outdated ideas
and generally colonial views of the Indian past, a totally banal
narrative and predictable illustrations of a poor quality.'[6]

Soon enough, in 1961, the NCERT (National Council of
Educational Research and Training) was set up. They formed a
committee to produce model textbooks that schools across the
country could use. The idea was that all the citizens of India
would study the same syllabus. In this sense, writing the social
science curriculum became a process of nationalization. It
was intended to create a shared and common identity. Romila
Thapar, along with some of the most prominent historians of
the time, including Bipan Chandra, Satish Chandra and R.S.
Sharma, wrote a series of textbooks that they claimed offered
a 'new way of looking at the past'; they 'critiqued colonial and
communal stereotypes and presented a history that was secular
and national'.[7] These books were model textbooks, and the
SCERTs (State Council of Educational Research and Training)
could adapt and model their own textbooks on these. Moreover,
anyone could now use this model syllabus and textbooks to
create their own. Perhaps, it was this very idea that had landed
me the opportunity to write textbooks for this private school.

At this juncture, it is important to note a critical feature of writing history and writing about history. The textbooks written by Thapar and other historians were a product of the socio-political circumstances of that time. It was the early 1960s, and the nationalist cause was very strong, with the nation rebuilding itself. It was within this context that the authors wanted to write books that reflected a secular, democratic and national culture. However, for whatever they achieved in working towards a secular and national cause, the books still failed to discuss the history of many of the social ills that plagued a hierarchical society. In Romila Thapar's own words, 'There was a hesitancy to analyze the inequities of caste or the degree to which the social articulation of religions formulated societies or failed to do so. Whereas colonial views of the recent past were critiqued, nationalist interpretation was less ready to critique the ancient Hindu past or the Islamic past, which were as much in need of critical analysis as the modern.'[8]

The politics of history textbooks closely mirrored and reflected the politics that has gone on to define India since its Independence. Ravaged by deadly communal violence before Independence and after it, two interpretations of history emerged. One was the attempt by professional historians, mostly trained in western universities, who sought to build a history of ancient and medieval India as one that was steeped in secularism, where people of different faiths and creeds mingled comfortably with each other, and which emphasized that the communalism of late was a recent and unfortunate phenomenon. Another branch of history was pioneered by the Hindu Right, which fiercely stuck to their ideas of India being a Hindu nation first and foremost and that India has repeatedly been invaded by intolerant, violent, ghoulish Muslim invaders. The Hindu Right also claimed that the textbooks that stressed on secularism had a 'Marxist imprint'. These two interpretations of history could hardly find common ground, and these textbooks became a huge bone of contention since the 1970s. Rightly so, textbooks were being contested as the future creators of an identity. What became the bones of contention were the ideas around identity and whose right it was to form it by interpreting the past.[9]

In 1969, members of the Parliamentary Consultative Committee wanted Romila Thapar's textbook to categorically state that the Aryans were indigenous to India, a claim that has for long formed the bulwark of Hindu right-wing ideology.[10] In 1977, when the coalition government of the Janata Party headed by Morarji Desai came to power, the Hindu Right forced the removal of the NCERT textbooks from circulation, calling the books anti-national and anti-Hindu.

In 1999, when the BJP government came to power, the tirade against textbooks went up a notch. Passages that were considered hurtful to Hindu religious sentiments were removed, particularly those related to beef eating and caste practices.[11] In 2004, the UPA government, headed by the Indian National Congress, promised to 'de-saffronize' the curriculum and appointed another committee to review the textbooks and suggest changes.[12] In 2012, the UPA government removed from the textbooks cartoons that were critical of Nehru. Since the government had overseen the creation of these texts a few years earlier, the removal of content resulted in many protests from leading academics and historians.[13] Clearly, chopping and changing the content of history textbooks was a game that all sorts of governments indulged in.

Peter Seixas, a historian and curriculum researcher, notes that a history curriculum does not only 'help to shape a group identity defined by common experience and belief' but also aids in understanding 'who is marginalized and who is excluded from the group'.[14]

While many governments have worked on rewriting history textbooks to suit their political narratives, current Hindu right-wing governments seek to recast Indian history as Hindu history at the cost of multiple other histories that have emerged in India. In 2021, a parliamentary committee recommended that 'Knowledge from the four Vedas—Sama Veda, Yajur Veda, Atharva Veda and Rig Veda—and the Bhagavad Gita should also be part of the syllabus'.[15] The committee added, 'NCERT and State Council for Educational Research and Training (SCERT) should incorporate the ancient wisdom, knowledge and teachings about life and society from Vedas and other great Indian texts/books in the school curriculum.' Another recent change brought in right after the pandemic removed all references to the 2002 Gujarat riots, while also drastically reducing content related to Mughal rule[16] and mentioning almost nothing about the history of caste in India.[17] The political science textbook also removed mention of the ban on the RSS after Nathuram Godse assassinated Gandhi.[18]

When the COVID-19 pandemic hit, the CBSE issued a dictum saying 'government-run schools no longer have to teach chapters on democratic rights, secularism, federalism, and citizenship, among other topics'.[19] Political scientist Christophe Jaffrelot argues that 'the nationalist tone of textbook rewriting deliberately extols ancient Indian knowledge systems over contemporary science.'[20]

I had reached out to some members of committees that had been involved with the NCERT in rewriting the social science curriculum and history textbooks over the last few decades. A former history professor involved in this process had much to say. 'Ever since the history textbook has emerged as a pedagogical tool, it has performed the task of building nations. That is nothing new. There is nothing particular or unique to India. All nation states want to control the textbook. With the rise of nation states, you have a very strong interest in what young students learn about the past,' said the professor over a telephonic interview. This rings true not just in an Indian context but across the world. In Russia, a specific history textbook described crimes, terror, and exploitation in the Soviet Union and asked Grade 10 students if they could assess Putin's style of leadership as an 'authoritarian dictatorship' and regime in Russia as a 'police state'. The reaction of President Putin was extremely negative. He stressed that history education should emphasize the great achievements of the nation and not its mistakes of wrong actions, pointing out that history textbooks 'should inculcate a feeling of pride for one's country'.[21]

A rudimentary analysis of history textbooks in western countries such as the US and the UK reveals that these countries deliberately construct narratives of war and paint themselves as the victim against the 'other' to construct an idea of unity and oneness. Some of the textbooks in the US that I accessed through some friends and the Internet depict heroic versions of incidents such as the Pearl Harbour, D-Day and other wars, showcasing the bravery of American troops. Similarly, some UK textbooks speak of Dunkirk, the defeat of Hitler and the heroics of Churchill. The horrors of colonialism and military conquests were conveniently forgotten until recently.

History textbooks and, by extension, the minds of young students, are now a battleground for the past. 'In the world, there are very few countries like India now where so many people are still interested in the past. The battle over the past is becoming so huge that it is becoming an all-consuming affair among different people. The number of non-professional historians who have entered the fray is huge,' said the Professor. 'I would say we are still trying to shake off our colonial past. It is deliberately addressing the white man to try and say we are great too. We have found ready support for this from NRIs across the world. What is happening is that there is an extraordinary amount of interest in Indian history from a very diverse group. There is very creative work going on. At the same time, there is an extraordinary paradox. The professional body of historians (viz., Indian Council of Historical Research or ICHR) has been extremely silent, and the narrative is being wrested and taken away, and that's what you are seeing in textbooks today. The difference with the Hindu Right narrative is that the end product is known.'

'Do you think it is time we rethink the textbook?' I asked.

'More than that, I think we need to rethink examinations. Textbooks prepare students for mass examinations. It makes history a process of obtaining nuggets of information,' they replied. 'Simply rewriting textbooks is not enough; we need to engage teachers, for they are the ones who are ultimately going to disseminate the information, and we need to rethink exams.'

Within a nationalist orientation of writing history for schoolchildren, larger aspects of sub-national history have been forgotten. 'Marginalized communities have been asking for a long time to include their histories. With the inclusion and research of more and more people, languages, and groups, we have a richer understanding of our past. But how does one communicate this past to school children?' they asked. 'All we can teach in schools is the historical method.'

The absence or, more recently, the intentional deletion of histories of marginalized communities, especially the most oppressed castes and women, has not escaped criticism. Many scholars have argued that understanding Indian society is only possible through an understanding of caste. However, the history of caste has barely found mention in schools' history textbooks.

Perhaps, the history of caste and oppression does not bode well for a nationalistic venture such as the history textbook. Romila Thapar, one of the authors of the first set of NCERT history textbooks, seemed to agree when I asked her about this in an e-mail. 'In any nationalist situation, there is a tendency not to be too critical of the positive rendering of the past. Nationalism requires legitimacy from history,' she said. However, a nationalistic attitude towards history risks excluding marginalized communities from forming a unified identity, mostly because their lived histories could be so different.

* * *

Over the course of a few months, I finished writing the textbook. After reading the first two chapters, which mentioned Nehru and the Partition, the director of the school lost interest in the project. He had stopped replying to my emails and stopped noticing if I was sitting at my designated desk in the office or not. I continued talking to teachers in the school, showing them some parts of the chapters and trying to take their inputs. Most teachers didn't seem interested; the others said they would comply if the school mandated it. I continued sending the director chapters for him to review until I finished all the nine chapters I had set out to write. The teachers continued doing what they were doing, their priority of completing the syllabus overwhelming them every step of the way.

Finally, on the last day of my contract, I went up to him with the compiled document and gave it to him.

'It's important to raise kids with patriotism and a proper idea of their past. Don't be so arrogant to think you can teach them other things,' he said, taking the compiled document and keeping it aside.

I walked out quietly, my head brimming with thoughts. Changing the world with a textbook would have to wait.

Conclusion

Who Deserves What?

'Sir, in Arani, we are going to be addressing a large gathering of women. This is going to be a sensitive issue,' said one of the political secretaries to the former higher education minister, whom I was travelling with on the campaign trail (in my role as a political consultant) before the Tamil Nadu Legislative Elections in 2021. Arani is a small town in northern Tamil Nadu and is known for its rice and, more recently, for its silk sarees and weavers. Having found relatively more wealth than other towns in the district, Arani appeared to sport a prosperous look, with big brands' showrooms selling clothes and electrical appliances.

The women were seated in chairs spread across a large wedding hall and were waiting impatiently. The former minister's cavalcade was late, and a lot of the women urgently had to return home. After the usual felicitations of different politicians, the minister asked the women to share their grievances and how a new government could help in local governance.

'Sir, what has the government ever done for us? You keep calling us to these meetings, give us biryani and ask for votes. I am a graduate; I have been looking for a job for a long time. But there are no jobs available. What is the point of all this education and the colleges you keep building?' asked a young woman. Her tone betrayed her frustration, which was further affirmed when the audience started clapping. The minister and his political aides were stunned into silence, and the grim mood in the hall was palpable. Here was a young woman who couldn't have possibly been over twenty-five, speaking to a stalwart of a prominent Tamil political party, expressing her frustration at something everyone appeared to have taken for granted.

What really was the point of the education she had received? She was a graduate, someone within only the 8.15 per cent[1] in India to have received a college education, but she wasn't able to find a job.

After the meeting was done, with several more complaints lodged against the state for doing nothing for its women and the bewildered former minister promising action, I approached the woman who had asked the question.

'What was your educational experience like?' I asked.

'Sir, I am not like you. I can't speak English like you. I studied in a government school nearby, and then I went to a government arts college in Tiruvannamalai. I don't have the kind of education you do,' she said, the frustration of the previous interaction still writ large on her face.

We came from vastly different educational backgrounds: mine was of privilege and hers was of accessing the only option available.

I was sent to an influential, yet affordable private CBSE school that had a reputation in the city for honing academically 'meritorious' students. My peers in the school were very similar in background and upbringing, with fathers who had white-collar jobs in the public or private sector and mothers who laboured tirelessly at home. Everyone lived within a 5-kilometre radius in similar neighbourhoods.

Throughout my school days, the academic aspect of the educational experience was rigorous. The need and desire to perform well in tests was inculcated from a very young age, and considering the kinds of privilege my peers and I enjoyed, most of us performed academically well. Those who didn't were quietly phased out from the school and asked to transfer to other institutions. In many ways, the school resembled the market. The high competition produced efficiency, and the inefficient were slowly weeded out. And in this situation, with us upper-caste students apparently having education as our only recourse to live in a society split into quotas by affirmative action, education became part of the marketplace. We had to compete in a global marketplace for skills and jobs. The women in Arani understood this, and that's why they asked the politicians their seething questions. The better you competed, the stronger your chances were of getting into good institutions and, ultimately, bagging well-paying jobs.

In 1991, on the cusp of a potential debt default and a balance-of-payment crisis, the Indian government decided to 'liberalize' the economy, opening much of its markets to private investment. While a detailed account of the effects and impacts of this economic liberalization is beyond the scope of this book, the vastly different educational experiences between the woman in Arani and me indicate a broader privatization of education. By this, I don't just mean the increase in private schools but also the engendering of an attitude that one's education was an individual, private affair. While I would not claim that the idea of markets is inherently bad or unjust, the marketization of education has led to severe political ramifications across the world. Scholars have noted that a neoliberal shift is well underway in different parts of the world with high-stakes standardized testing, rigid curricula, reduction of teachers to the position of labour, elimination of teacher unions and, in India, the exponential rise in private schools.[2]

Neoliberalism has prompted citizens to pursue education to be socially and economically capable and participate in the global processes of capital formation. We have moved from being a bearer of rights to a consumer of 'educational services' through markets.

I remember a math teacher in school who kept telling my parents and me that I had to work harder and get better marks, for if I didn't, there would be no suitable opportunities. It was a formative time, and continuous reinforcement of this narrative from multiple quarters made it unquestionable and a self-evident truth.

Perhaps, what this teacher said was applicable to me, but from my experience of writing this book, or even from that conversation with that woman in Arani, this was a narrative broadly discussed in neoliberal India. Today, this continuous peddling of a narrative of self-reliance—that we are responsible for ourselves and our actions—often betrays the malnourished and undereducated reality of the hundreds of millions of Indians, who continuously hear rallying cries of freedom and self-reliance but know deep down that they can't compete in global markets. Moreover, psychological studies on the effects of neoliberalism have shown that it enforces an 'individualist-entrepreneurial understanding of the self.'[3] Some scholars have also suggested that individuals have been reconfigured as 'economic-entrepreneurs' and institutions have been redesigned to be capable of producing these 'economic-entrepreneurs'. At the heart of this exceptionalist and individualistic enterprise lies the school, whose policies, curricula and pedagogy continuously reinforce the notion of individualism. Within these ambits, the individual comes to understand themselves as free, supposedly capable of completely governing themselves, while subject to invisible conditions beyond their control.

A particular feature of neoliberal subjects is that their desires, hopes, ideals and fears have been shaped so that they desire to be morally worthy, responsible individuals who, as successful entrepreneurs, can produce the best for themselves and their families.[4] This attains a dimension of creating a lifestyle for oneself, perhaps unimaginable before the Indian neoliberal era. Neoliberal policies, with the emphasis on creating such individuals, have also shaped a consumption lifestyle, with the adage that 'more is good', not just for themselves or the family but for society too. Within this consumption dimension lies this fantasy that if you work hard and play by the rules, you too can one day become rich and rise up in society in the right way.

The Middle Class

While growing up, I heard the word 'middle class' at home and at school. The term, I think is something of a buzzword. I say this because it is a term that has been appropriated by Indians of various demographics, castes, classes and genders to peddle narratives that have suited them. The term 'rich' was never appropriate to use, at home or at school, for it then took away the legitimacy of a largely monotonous and laborious education. 'We are middle class; we cannot afford to buy seats or send you abroad, so the only way out for you is to score well.' This is what I was continuously told. It was implicit in every conversation, every parent-teacher meeting and every time I scored badly in exams (which was a little too often for anyone's liking).

For more than two decades now, India has seen rapid change and growth. We see swanky shopping malls and tall IT parks; we see the overt flamboyance in our film industries and stories of 'successful' Indians. Amidst these largely visible and hyped-up changes, a stark contrast to the age of the 'Licence-Raj' during which India grew slowly and jobs were scarce, a narrative highlighting the emergence of the middle class has surfaced, showcasing a new cohort of educated consumers in India with purchasing power and proficiency in the English language, alongside various other defining characteristics.

As my father started earning more, investing more and rising in his organization, there was a perceivable change in our material well-being. Was I no longer part of the middle class? Had we become part of the rich upper class? My father soon sold his first car, a Maruti 800, and bought a sedan; we moved into a bigger house within a gated community, and we made a few international trips. However, the narrative now was that I was part of the expanding middle class, the section of the population that would drive the next few decades of growth and consumption.

But what is this middle class, and how is one to define it and, more importantly, how is it produced, reproduced and who really is the middle class? Was being part of the middle class an economic construct based on how much one earned or spent or did it go beyond to signify social and cultural constructs as well? These are questions that economists and sociologists across the world have spent years working on, with very different conclusions and takeaways.

In his book *Muscular India,*[5] Michiel Baas brings out the befuddling enterprise of calculating the exact number of the middle-class population in India. He notes that the number has been pegged at 300 million for a long time. Many scholars have come up with different numbers. Political scientist Leela Fernandes[6] cited a 250-million-strong middle-class population, while Amita Baviskar and Raka Ray[7] write that 'the top 26 per cent' of Indian households belong to this income group. In 2010, Homi Kharas[8] of the Brookings Institution estimated that about 380 million Indians—with per capita incomes between $11 and $110 (in purchasing power parity terms) per person per day in 2011 (equivalent to Rs 171 and Rs 1714)—would enter the middle class between 2015 and 2022. In 2012, the Centre for Global Development estimated that India's middle class would be around 100 million.[9] Based on the National Survey on Household Income and Expenditure conducted by the National Council for Applied Economics Research (NCAER), which defines the middle class as those with household incomes between Rs two lakh and Rs ten lakh per annum, Rajesh Shukla estimated India's middle class to be 153 million in 2010.[10] But all these numbers also indicate then that over a billion people in India are not middle-class but lower.

In her illuminating portrait on Indian data, *Whole Numbers and Half Truths*,[11] Rukmini S. reveals multiple aspects of who is poor and who is 'middle-class in India'. She reveals that in a nationally representative household survey conducted in 2014, more than 50 per cent of the rich identify as middle class, and over 40 per cent of the poor also identify as middle class. She further notes that a nationally representative household survey conducted by the National Statistics Organization on consumption expenditure shows that the average Indian spends a little under Rs 2500 every month. It also revealed that anyone in urban India who spends more than Rs 8500 a month would be in the top 5 per cent of the country. As Rukmini argues in her book, look around you and think about how many people can actually afford to spend Rs 8500 a month and these numbers will start making sense. If consumption expenditure is one aspect of calculating who belongs to the middle class, the data on income reveals something even more befuddling. If we were to divide Indians into five classes of income equally, Rukmini calculates that the middle 20 per cent of Indian households would earn Rs 55,000 to Rs 88,000 annually. This amounts to a monthly income between Rs 4600 and Rs 7300 per household. Based on this data, we can conclude that whoever belongs to the middle class in India is, in many ways, very poor. These numbers, however, only point to one aspect of poverty. India is battling what the World Bank also refers to as 'Learning Poverty',[12] which means being unable to read and understand a simple text by age ten.

Foundational Literacy and Numeracy Crisis

Behind the Indian dream of going to school, studying well and increasing one's economic prospects lie many dark but open secrets. By the dawn of the new century, and going forward, the Indian state had achieved something monumental. The gross enrolment ratio of kids in primary education was almost at 100 per cent in most states (it was more in every state until the pandemic), which basically meant that almost every child in India was at least going to primary school.[13] At the same time, India was witnessing unprecedented growth, with the economy trying to make a serious push into the service sector. Cities such as Bangalore and Gurgaon started witnessing exponential growth on the back of high demand for service sector jobs, and many multinational companies were investing in India. Among many other factors, this played a significant role in my life as I finished high school just as a tech boom was entering India. My seniors in school and my older cousins were all landing plum jobs with huge pay cheques. 'There are opportunities everywhere; if you work hard and stay focused, you can do whatever you want,' said a professor during one of the first weeks of my mechanical engineering degree. Perhaps, it was meant as a motivational speech for students from all walks of life. But privilege plays its part like it always does. During campus placements, it was mainly the privileged, CBSE-educated, English-speaking students who landed the service sector jobs with seven-digit pay packages.

That India has a learning problem is a fact everyone knows but no one acknowledges. One of India's largest educational NGOs, Pratham, has been measuring learning outcomes in India's schools since 2005 and the results are astonishing, as seen in their Annual Status of Education Reports (ASER).[14] In 2022, only 42.8 per cent of all children in Class 5 in government and private schools in India could read a Class 2-level text. Moreover, there has been a steady decline in these reading levels from 2008 to 2018. In 2008, 53.1 per cent of all children in Class 5 of government schools in India could read a Class 2-level text, but in 2018, that number was down to 44.2 per cent, and in 2022, the number is at 42.8 per cent.

These numbers become worse when it comes to numeracy. In 2022, only 25.6 per cent of all children in Class 5 of government schools could do division, and just like the literacy levels, these numbers have shown a steady decline as well. In 2008, 34.4 per cent of all children in Class 5 of government schools could do division.

There are, of course, regional variations, with some states such as Himachal Pradesh, Punjab, Maharashtra and Tamil Nadu doing relatively better than the others. But the fact of the matter remains that children are going to school and not learning much. As mentioned by the founder of Pratham, Madhav Chavan, 'not only are we not creating a sufficiently literate population, but that most of our population is functionally illiterate'.[15] An analysis of ASER[16] at an all-India level from 2008 to 2022 shows that while children did learn as they progressed through school, these learning trajectories were flat. Even by the time children came to Class 8, only 44.7 per cent of all children in government schools could do division.

In a report published by the Central Square Foundation (CSF) on private schools in India,[17] it was estimated that 120 million students study in private schools in India, making it almost half the Indian school student population. Considered independently, the private school ecosystem with 120 million students and 4,50,000 schools makes up the world's third largest school system after China and India's public school system. On analysing Indian government data on school enrolment between public and private schools, CSF found out that the proportion of students attending private schools has grown rapidly over the last fifty years.

Between 1973 and 2017, enrolments in private unaided schools grew thirty-three times. This trend further spilled on to rural private schools as well. In 1993, only 4 per cent of children in rural areas went to private schools. By 2018, it was almost 27 per cent. In urban areas, around 73 per cent of all children study in private schools. By this time, it was clear that parents and students were voting with their feet. Despite children having almost universal access to free education provided by the state, they were moving to private schools. While arriving at a particular causality for this phenomenon might be very difficult, one can guess that the perceived failures of public schools in providing quality education could be a reason for this increased demand.

Children in private schools in India do better than their public-school peers, but it is not as if their performance is exemplary. In 2018, 65.1 per cent of all children in Class 5 of private schools in India could read a Class 2-level text, while only 39.8 per cent could divide a three-digit number by a single digit.[18] Despite this, what has emerged is a phenomenon that is here to stay: the rise and dominance of private schools in India.

Furthermore, the highly industrialized and developed states in India, including Tamil Nadu, Maharashtra, Haryana, Gujarat and Punjab, all report more than 50 per cent private school enrolment.[19] These numbers have dropped after the COVID-19 pandemic, but private school enrolment still remains high. Within all of this, there are high variances depending on the student's urban or rural location, household income and even school fees. What is clear from the above data is that sending children to school is not enough; there is copious amounts of work left to be done in improving foundational literacy and numeracy skills.

The Politics and Purpose of Education

Within this din around educational access, quality and equity in opportunities to seek education lies an important debate about who deserves what. Firm affirmative action in India, with jobs and educational seats reserved for people from historically marginalized sections of Indian society, has caused severe distress within the dominant castes, the middle class and the privileged, who often feel there is no scope for them to work within the system. The school I studied in reinforced that belief. Once I was in high school, the narrative appeared to change suddenly, as if a rug was pulled from beneath your feet. Until middle school, the focus was on academics, but the pressure was relatively low. But in high school, the narrative that the dominant castes have no place anywhere within the system and that private markets for education were the only way to escape the 'tyranny' of the quota system in India became an everyday topic. Worried parents huddled around each other discussing options and astronomical private university fees; teachers put more effort into the more meritorious students, and the few serious students doubled down on their efforts to score better to ensure they could still get into top-notch institutions within the system. The beleaguered rest decided that none of this made sense, knowing that their parents would figure a way out.

While it is beyond the scope of this chapter to discuss the effects of affirmative action on various caste groups in India, I have brought it up to show the gross inequality in educational quality across the country and if one can argue that everyone is on a level playing field, and if education really provides that. By continuously peddling the myth of meritocracy in a neoliberalized world where opportunities are getting farther and farther out of reach, the politics of education becomes a politics of humiliation, where regret and comparisons are constantly provoked. This is evident in the number of suicides seen every year in India's premier educational institutions, including the IITs. The politics of affirmative action aside, the politics of education in India is a politics of humiliation, primarily because a small group of people are being educated to reap the benefits of hyper-globalization and can consider themselves economic-entrepreneurs, while a very large group of people are being left defenceless to the expansion of markets due to a massive learning crisis, amongst a whole host of other factors.

As Zygmunt Bauman points out, '[T]he most consequential dimension of the planetary-wide expansion of [neoliberal capital] has been the slow yet relentless globalization of the production of human waste, or more precisely "wasted humans"—humans no longer necessary for the completion of the economic cycle and thus impossible to accommodate within a social framework resonant with the capitalist economy.'[20]

If the economic situation were different, the kind of education, the pedagogy and ideas on the politics and purposes of education would have been different. The politics of education and, by extension, the purpose of education, has now come to largely rely on a neoliberal, global market-based order.

Solutions to solve the vast problems of education in India are diverse and are being handled by some of the best in the world. Economists and sociologists in the best universities, seasoned bureaucrats, committed teachers and well-informed civil society organizations are doing excellent and contextual work. But it is at this juncture that we require a rethinking of our notions of success, merit and the purpose of education. What do we educate for, and whose needs are served by education? I hope that continuous thinking on these questions will one day bring forth a critical questioning of education, its purpose and, more importantly, its negative effects.

Education achieves a lot of things; it pulls people out of poverty; it gives people the opportunity to be socially and economically mobile, among so many other important objectives. Through the stories in this book, I hope to have shed light on the effect that education has on some social dynamics in India, and its ability to bridge differences while simultaneously creating new ones. Education can bridge many differences, but in its current form, it creates one very important difference—a new class of people: the smart and the dumb. The smart, who can stay ahead of the game in this complex, globalizing world, while the dumb have to stay behind, because they 'deserve' their fate. The politics of education then becomes a politics of humiliation, antithetical to the promise of education where education was supposed to provide dignity and recognition. As the political philosopher Thomas Nagel once said, 'When racial and sexual injustice have been reduced, we shall still be left with the grave injustice of the smart and the dumb.'[21]

Acknowledgements

This book has stayed with me for a long six years, and as I look at the ever-evolving list of people to thank, I find myself caught between feeling immense relief and gratitude. The ideas, the stories and the narrative accrued over time, with insights that seemed heretical at first and gospel later. These insights accrued from my fellow travellers, my *musafirs*, but also from hard-nosed sceptics, the curious, and, at times, the uninterested. This acknowledgement thus becomes not just a public expression of gratitude but also a testament to the collaborative effort that shaped this book, in content and spirit, even if the credit often unfairly appears to rest solely with the author.

My gratitude is due first to my erudite and sharp editor, Karthik Venkatesh at Penguin Random House India, who not only brought a very rough manuscript to shape but initially saw the promise in these stories. Thank you for believing in me.

The idea that a project like this could even be possible was affirmed and validated by Krishna Trilok six years ago, who first told me that this is something worth pursuing. I owe my gratitude to my dear friend and philosopher, Dr Ashwin Krishnan, who over the years, has patiently engaged in my dilemmas.

This book involved a considerable amount of travel, and it could not have happened without the guidance and benevolence of many people. I am indebted to Ram Pappu and Akther Ghori at Mission Samriddhi, who introduced me to amazing work happening across the country; their introductions shaped my travel, and consequently, the stories I wrote.

To Sanjana Yadav, for her help and so much more in writing the first chapter, and to Tejaram Mali and Punaramji for taking a young, curious soul under their wings in Tilonia and Govardhanpura and showing me around.

To M, whose relentless energy, compassion and understanding of Manipur has shaped my work in so many ways, and to R and Ishaan, whose delightful company kept me sane.

To Rajesh, Yesthov, Kotpandi Raju, Arul Yenbaraj and the many other palmyra tree climbers who patiently answered my questions, and fed me enough karupatti that I couldn't eat anything sweet for weeks. And to my dear friend and collaborator, Dr Vignesh Karthik KR, for all the long discussions on Dravidian politics, often extending to palm trees.

To the Madras Dyslexia Association, especially Lata, Lakshmi and D. Chandrasekar for the introductions to my interlocutors and for taking many lessons for me on ADHD, dyslexia and autism. Many women, mothers of children with ADHD and/or autism shared their stories enthusiastically with me, and I am humbled and incredibly grateful for their trust.

To Malu, who looked at me with disbelief when I said I was cancelling my trip to Kota and dragged me to the railway station, and for providing me with a roof over my head in Delhi for weeks.

To my many interlocutors in Chennai schools for answering me beyond my questions.

The Harvard Graduate School of Education is a wonderful space, for it rigorously trained its students to be compassionate educators, while sowing seeds of intellectual curiosity. My friends and professors, with whom I continue to have the most enriching conversations about education and life, have shaped this book in many unsaid ways.

At Harvard, I had the privilege of Dr Suraj Yengde's friendship, whose many bowls of delicious dal and insights nourished my body and work.

My sincere gratitude to my friends who read different drafts of this book, in part or in full, for dealing with my obsessions and moods: Tarun Karthikeyan, Shreya Agarwal, Bhargav Prasad, Smitha TK, Barath Balaji, Roshni Sathish, Jaiveer Johal, Sriram Sundarraj and Dhruva Bhat.

To my partner, Akshaya, who read and re-read every chapter, travelled with me on most journeys for this book and provided space over many years for my ideas to emerge. Your friendship, love and critique have fostered a nurturing environment for my work and being. Like everything else, this book is as much yours as it is mine.

To my parents, Lata and Vasanth, who have watched my meanderings with bewilderment and love, and for infusing every journey of mine with hope and belief.

And finally, to my friend Vinesh, whose life was an education in living with dignity, joy and love. I will always remember you.

Notes

Introduction

1 Research on globalization and inequality is vast, with scholars from different disciplines undertaking research to show how globalization has led to inequality. Thomas Piketty's *Capital in the Twenty-First Century* (2014) and *Capital and Ideology* (2019) illustrate this phenomenon in detail. To understand globalization and educational inequality, also see Lall, M., and Nambissan, G.B. (eds.). (2020). *Education and Social Justice in the Era of Globalization: Perspectives from India and the UK.* (Taylor & Francis).

2 See the U-DISE report by the Government of India: https://www.education.gov.in/sites/upload_files/mhrd/files/statistics-new/udise_21_22.pdf.
Also see the budget note: https://www.indiabudget.gov.in/economicsurvey/doc/stat/tab83.pdf. I have broadly paraphrased the material presented in multiple pages of this article.

3 See Stephen Ball's introduction in Ball, S.J., Dworkin, A.G., and Vryonides, M. (2010). 'Globalization and Education: Introduction,' *Current Sociology*, *58*(4), pp. 523–29.

4 See Walter Powell and Keisa Snellman's article on Knowledge Economy. Powell, W.W., and Snellman, K. (2004). 'The Knowledge Economy', *Annu. Rev. Sociol.*, *30*, pp. 199–220.

5 World Bank (2003). *Lifelong Learning in the Global Knowledge Economy: Challenges for Developing Countries.* Washington, DC.

I have broadly paraphrased the material presented from multiple pages in this report.

6 See Freire, P., *Pedagogy of the Oppressed.* (Penguin Classics. 2017). I have broadly paraphrased the material presented from multiple pages in this book.

Chapter 1: 'The Girl Will Get Away'

1 Eric Fromm, *The Heart of Man: Its Genius for Good and Evil* (Routledge & K. Paul, 1965), p. 32.

2 P. Freire, *Pedagogy of the Oppressed.* (Penguin Classics, 2017).

3 'Annual Status of Education Report (Rural) 2022', *ASER*, January 2023, pp. 50–51, https://img.asercentre.org/docs/ASER%202022%20report%20pdfs/All%20India%20documents/aserreport2022.pdf.

Chapter 2: Guns for Christmas

1 Urvashi Butalia, *The Other Side of Silence: Voices from the Partition of India* (Penguin Random House India, 2017), p. 8.

2 See M.S. Prabhakara, 'Burdens of the Past', *Frontline*, 9 September 2004, https://frontline.thehindu.com/cover-story/article30224476.ece.

3 See A. Roychowdhury, 'How Manipur Merged with India: From a Constitutional Monarchy to Part C State', the *Indian Express*, 26 August 2023, https://indianexpress.com/article/research/how-manipur-merged-with-india-from-a-constitutional-monarchy-to-part-c-state-8888978/.

4 See A. Sufian, 'Geopolitics of the NRC-CAA in Assam: Impact on Bangladesh–India Relations', *Asian Ethnicity*, *23*(3), (2022), pp. 556–86.

5 See the Armed Forces (Special Powers) Act, 1958, particularly Section 4a of the act, https://www.mha.gov.in/sites/default/files/armed_forces_special_powers_act1958.pdf.

6   Krishnandas Rajagopal, 'Manorama "Mercilessly Tortured"', *The Hindu,* 14 November 2014, https://www.thehindu. com/news/national/manorama-death-brutal-torture-probe-panel/article6596278.ece.

7   Simrin Sirur, '17 Years Since Their Naked Protest Against Army, "Mothers of Manipur" Say Fight Not Over Yet,' ThePrint, 22 July 2021, https://theprint.in/india/17-years-since-their-naked-protest-against-army-mothers-of-manipur-say-fight-not-over-yet/700093/.

8   See P. Kirby, 'The Body Weaponized: War, Sexual Violence and the Uncanny', *Security Dialogue*, *51*(2–3), (2020), pp. 211–30, https://doi.org/10.1177/0967010619895663;

—Z. H. Bangura, and M. Verveer, 'Sexual Violence Is a Tool of War, but We Have the Weapons to End That', the *Guardian*, 19 October 2022, https://www.theguardian.com/global-development/2016/mar/02/sexual-violence-is-a-tool-of-war-but-we-have-the-weapons-to-end-that;

—For usage of rape as a weapon in war in India, see Human Rights Watch, 'Rape in Kashmir: A Crime of War', https://www.hrw.org/sites/default/files/reports/INDIA935.PDF

9   S. Baruah, *In the Name of the Nation: India and its Northeast* (Stanford University Press, 2020).

10   See M. Khan, 'State and Ethnic Violence in Manipur: A Multilateral Federation of Territories and Cultures for Peace', *The Indian Journal of Political Science*, 67(3), (2006), pp. 429–42;

—K. Mukherjee, (2017), 'Insurgency and Peace Building in the Northeast Indian State of Manipur', *Democracy and Security*, 13(3), pp. 220-245;

—S. Baruah, *In the Name of the Nation: India and its Northeast.* I have broadly paraphrased the material presented from multiple pages in these articles.

11   NSCN stood for the National Socialist Council of Nagaland, and the various letters appended to it referred to the different factions. NNC was the Naga National Council. GPRN was

the Government of the People's Republic of Nagaland established by the NSCN-IM. FGN was the Federal Government of Nagaland. UNLF was the United National Liberation Front. PLA was the People's Liberation Army. KCP was the Kangleipak Communist Party.

12 Manipur Official Language Act 1979, https://www. indiacode.nic.in/bitstream/123456789/13438/1/the_ manipur_official_language_act%2c_1979.pdf

13 For the sake of brevity, I have had to generalize and paraphrase a lot of historical nuances about the Meitei, Kuki and Naga movements. For more on Meitei disaffection, who happen to be Hindu and having ceded into an India that is also largely Hindu, see N. Chandhoke (2006), 'A State of One's Own: Secessionism and Federalism in India', Working Paper No. 80, Crisis State Programme, LSE, London, https://eprints. lse.ac.uk/28146/1/wp80.pdf; Also, see S.S. Hanjabam, 'The Meitei Upsurge in Manipur', *Asia Europe Journal*, 6(1), (2008), pp. 157–69.

14 Almost twenty years later, a trial court found two people guilty and sentenced them to life imprisonment, https:// thefrontiermanipur.com/lungnila-elizabeth-case-two-sentenced-to-life-imprisonment/a.
Coverage about the event can be found here: https://www. theguardian.com/world/2003/nov/13/india.maseehrahman.

15 See M. Sitlhou, 'Accord', *Fifty Two*, 3 December 2020, https://fiftytwo.in/story/accord/ and Karan Thapar's interview with Th. Muivah, https://www.youtube.com/ watch?v=kAz04Q6lm3E; Also see S. Baruah, *In the Name of the Nation: India and its Northeast*. I have broadly paraphrased the material presented from multiple pages in this article.

16 See Chapter 4 in S. Baruah, *In the Name of the Nation: India and its Northeast*. I have broadly paraphrased the material presented from multiple pages in this book.

17 There are many accounts of this, with some claiming that Nehru insisted on resolving Naga revolts peacefully and some claiming that it was a brutal military campaign designed to quell the uprising. A useful account of this turbulent period can be found here: S. Nag, 'Nehru and the Nagas: Minority Nationalism and the Post-Colonial State', *Economic and Political Weekly*, *44*(49), (2009), pp. 48–55, http://www.jstor.org/stable/25663861.

18 Sharma, L., De, S., Kandpal, P., Olaniya, M.P., Yadav, S., Bhardwaj, T., Thorat, P., Panja, S., Arora, P., Sharma, N., Agarwal, A., Senguttuvan, T.D., Ojha, V.N., and Aswal, D.K. (2018). 'Necessity of "Two Time Zones: IST-I (UTC + 5 : 30 h) and IST-II (UTC + 6 : 30 h)" in India and its Implementation', *Current Science*, *115*(7), pp. 1252–61. https://www.jstor.org/stable/26978397;

Also see Lakshmi Supriya, 'Two Timezones in India Could Make Country's Northeast More Productive: Study', The Wire, 15 October 2018, https://thewire.in/the-sciences/two-timezones-in-india-could-make-countrys-northeast-more-productive-study.

19 T. Harad, 'ST Status for Manipur's Meiteis: What Is at Stake?', The Quint, 6 May 2023, https://www.thequint.com/news/politics/manipur-violence-st-status-for-meiteis-valley-vs-hills.

20 Some details about the event can be found here: https://thewire.in/rights/chassad-sampui-manipur.   Also   see: https://www.thesangaiexpress.com/Encyc/2020/3/17/Mungchan-ZimikUkhrul-Mar-16-Villa-gers-of-Kamjong-torched-around-150-houses-belong-ing-to-Chassad-village-under-Kamjong-district-today-following-a-land-dispute-between-Sampui-and-Chassad-village-.html.

21 J. J. Wouters and M. Heneise (eds.), *Nagas in the 21st Century* (Highlander Books, 2017). I have broadly paraphrased the material presented from multiple pages in this book.

22 Asojini Rachel Kashena, 'Prayers from the Kuki-Naga Conflict: Living through Violence in Manipur', *The South Asianist*, 5(1), (2017). I have broadly paraphrased the material presented from multiple pages in this article.

23 K. Theidon, 'The Mask and the Mirror: Facing up to the Past in Postwar Peru', *Anthropologica*, 48(1), (2006), pp. 87–100. https://doi.org/10.2307/25605299.

24 See G. Petonito, 'Racial Discourse and Enemy Construction', *Social Conflicts and Collective Identities*, 20–40, (2000).

Chapter 3: Tap That Toddy

1 Hanne Marlene Dahl Fraser, Pauline Stoltz, and Rasmus Willig, 'Recognition, Redistribution and Representation in Capitalist Global Society: An Interview with Nancy Fraser', *Acta Sociologica*, 47(4), (2004), pp. 374–82, https://doi.org/10.1177/000169930404867.

2 See Madras High Court's judgment, https://www.mhc.tn.gov.in/judis/index.php/casestatus/viewpdf/541354. Also see 'Enumerate and Enlist All Unorganised Workers in 34 Welfare Boards, HC Directs Government', *The Hindu*, 27 August 2020, https://www.thehindu.com/news/national/tamil-nadu/enumerate-and-enlist-all-unorganised-workers-in-34-welfare-boards-hc-directs-govt/article32460511.ece.

3 For a detailed understanding of the Nadars' association with palmyra tree climbing, see M.S.S. Pandian, 'Caste in Tamil Nadu: A History of Nadar Censorship', *Economic and Political Weekly*, (2013), pp. 12–14.

4 Details about the Nadar Mahajana Sangam can be found here: R. L. Hardgrave, 'Varieties of Political Behavior among Nadars of Tamilnad,' *Asian Survey*, 6(11), (1966), pp. 614–21, https://doi.org/10.2307/2642284.

5   Quoted from R. L. Hardgrave, 'Varieties of Political Behavior among Nadars of Tamilnad'.

6   See Mridula Char, 'The Long and Twisted History of Prohibition in Tamil Nadu', Scroll, 11 April 2016, https:// scroll.in/article/806448/the-long-and-twisted-history-of-prohibition-in-tamil-nadu; Vignesh Karthik K.R and C.R. Kesavan, 'Comment: Tamil Nadu's Liquor Conundrum', *The Hindu*, 18 May 2020, https://www.thehindu.com/ news/national/tamil-nadu/tamil-nadus-liquor-conundrum/ article31610374.ece; M.G. Devasahayam, 'The Politics of Prohibition in Tamil Nadu', The Wire, 15 April 2016, https://thewire.in/government/the-politics-of-prohibition-in-tamil-nadu.

7   https://thewire.in/government/the-politics-of-prohibition-in-tamil-nadu.

8   See the excise minister's statement on this in 'Tamil Nadu Sees a Rise in Liquor Sale Revenue Last Fiscal,' the *Indian Express*, 23 April 2023, https://indianexpress.com/article/ cities/chennai/tamil-nadu-sees-a-rise-in-liquor-sale-revenue-last-fiscal-8554082/; for a complete transcript of the Finance Minister's budget speech, see https://www.tn.gov.in/ documents/category/4.

9   P. Jeffery and R. Jeffery, *Degrees Without Freedom?* (Stanford University Press, 2007). I have broadly paraphrased the material presented from multiple pages in this book.

10   Ibid.

11   A detailed list of every college and relevant statistics is available at the website of the All India Survey on Higher Education: https://www.aishe.gov.in/aishe/home. For a list of engineering colleges in Tamil Nadu, see TNEA's booklet, https://static.tneaonline.org/docs/TNEA20_Booklet.pdf.

12   C.J. Fuller and H. Narasimhan, 'Engineering Colleges, "Exposure" and Information Technology: Professionals in Tamil Nadu', *Economic and Political Weekly*, (2006), pp. 258–88.

13 See G.B. Nambissan, 'The Indian Middle Classes and Educational Advantage: Family Strategies and Practices', *The Routledge International Handbook of the Sociology of Education*, (2010), pp. 303–13, https://doi.org/10.4324/9780203863701-34. I have broadly paraphrased the material presented from multiple pages in this article.

14 Ibid. Also see G.B. Nambissan, 'Equity in Education? Schooling of Dalit Children in India', *Economic and Political Weekly*, (1996), pp. 1011–24.

15 See 'District Wise Skill Gap Study for the State of Tamil Nadu (2012–17, 2017–22), National Skill Development Corporation,' https://skillsip.nsdcindia.org/sites/default/files/kps-document/Tamil%20Nadu%20Skill%20Gap%20Report.pdf. I have broadly paraphrased the material presented from multiple pages in this article.

16 A. Kalaiyarasan and M. Vijayabaskar, *The Dravidian Model: Interpreting the Political Economy of Tamil Nadu* (Cambridge University Press, 2021).

17 Ibid.

18 'Palm Tree Workers Board Gets New Lease of Life a Decade Later', the *New Indian Express*, 19 June 2022, https://www.newindianexpress.com/states/tamil-nadu/2022/jun/19/palm-tree-workers-board-gets-new-lease-of-life-a-decade-later-2467357.html.

Chapter 4: To Enter Entrance Exams

1 Max Weber, *Essays in Sociology*, Part III, 'Religion', Chapter XI, 'The Social Psychology of the World Religions' (Oxford University Press, 1946), p. 271.

2 See the website of Allen, the coaching centre mentioned where they have put up news of the world record: https://myexam.allen.ac.in/more-than-1-25-lakh-classroom-students-registered-at-allen-kota/.

3   'Kota, India Metro Area Population 1950–2023', https://www.macrotrends.net/cities/21310/kota/population.

4   The National Testing Agency (NTA) puts out an official notification every year with the total number of registrations. It can be found at *www.nta.ac.in*.

5   A detailed seat matrix of how many seats are available in each IIT can be found on the website of the Joint Seat Allocation Authority, https://josaa.admissions.nic.in/applicant/seatmatrix/seatmatrixinfo.aspx.

6   It is estimated that Allen, the biggest coaching centre in Kota alone, clocked revenue of Rs 1600 crore in 2019 to 2020, 'ALLEN: Maheshwari Brothers of Kota Have Built a Coaching Empire Brick by Brick', Prashant K. Nanda, 2 May 2022, https://www.moneycontrol.com/news/business/companies/allen-maheshwari-brothers-of-kota-have-built-a-coaching-empire-brick-by-brick-8442941.html; Also see 'Kota's Coaching Centres Are Back in Full Swing, Operating in Hybrid Mode', Prachi Verma, 13 May 2022, https://economictimes.indiatimes.com/industry/services/education/kotas-coaching-centres-are-back-in-full-swing-operating-in-hybrid-mode/articleshow/91531357.cms?from=mdr.

7   See A. Subramanian, *The Caste of Merit* (Harvard University Press, 2019), https://doi.org/10.4159/9780674243477. I have broadly paraphrased the material presented from multiple pages in this book.

8   As mentioned in the Narayana group's website: https://www.narayanagroup.com/about-us.

9   See R. Lamba and A. Subramanian, 'Dynamism with Incommensurate Development: The Distinctive Indian Model', *Journal of Economic Perspectives*, 34(1), (2020), pp. 3–30.

10 See Samarth Bansal and Pramit Bhattacharya, 'How Privilege Shapes Learning Outcomes in India', 22 January 2019, https://www.livemint.com/politics/policy/how-privilege-shapes-learning-outcomes-in-india-1548086593289.html.

11 Read the full minutes here: https://www.iitsystem.
    ac.in/sites/default/files/councilminutes/minutes/49/
    bfef92be7836d3a79571e9b4b88db.pdf.

12 Ibid., p. 4 and p. 5. The report from the meeting no longer
    exists but was previously accessed from https://www.
    education.gov.in/49th-meeting-council-iits-iit-bombay-0.

13 S. Deshpande, 'Pass, Fail, Distinction: The Examination
    as a Social Institution', Third Marjorie Sykes Memorial
    Lecture delivered at the Regional Institute of Education,
    Ajmer, (2010), https://www.academia.edu/36917384/Pass_
    Fail_Distinction_The_Examination_as_a_Social_Institution.

14 See Satish Deshpande's papers on this topic, including:
    —S. Deshpande and Y. Yadav, 'Redesigning Affirmative
    Action: Castes and Benefits in Higher Education', *Economic
    and Political Weekly*, (2006), pp. 2419–24.
    —S. Deshpande, 'Exclusive Inequalities: Merit, Caste and
    Discrimination in Indian Higher Education Today', *Economic
    and Political Weekly* (2006): pp. 2438–44.
    —S. Deshpande, 'Pass, Fail, Distinction: The Examination as
    a Social Institution', Third Marjorie Sykes Memorial Lecture
    delivered at the Regional Institute of Education, Ajmer,
    (2010).

15 See M.J. Sandel, *The Tyranny of Merit: What's Become of the
    Common Good?* (United Kingdom: Penguin, 2020). I have
    broadly paraphrased the material presented from multiple
    pages in this book.

Chapter 5: A Good Mother

1   M. Foucault and A. Sheridan, 'Discipline and Punish: The
    Birth of the Prison / Michel Foucault', translated from the
    French by Alan Sheridan (Harmondsworth: Penguin Books,
    1991).

2   See R. Banerji and W. Wadhwa, *The COVID Effect: Changing Patterns in Public and Private Inputs into Schooling in Rural India*, (2021). Retrieved from https://img.asercentre.org/docs/aser2021-commentary.pdf.

3   The literature on the side-effects of ADHD medication is vast and increasing. Some studies I was pointed to by Zakhif include S.L. Toomey, C.M. Sox, D. Rusinak and J.A. Finkelstein, 'Why Do Children with ADHD Discontinue Their Medication?' *Clinical Pediatrics*, *51*(8), (2012), pp. 763–69, https://doi.org/10.1177/0009922812446744 and M.S. Gordon and G.A. Melvin, 'Do Antidepressants Make Children and Adolescents Suicidal?' *Journal of Paediatrics and Child Health*, *50*(11), (2014), pp. 847–54.

Chapter 6: Performance of Culture

1   P. Bourdieu, 'Outline of a Theory of Practice', *Cambridge Studies in Social Anthropology* (Cambridge University Press, 1977).

2   The terms 'social capital' and 'cultural capital' are borrowed from Pierre Bourdieu's framework. His work remains deeply influential in the study of how inequalities are reproduced and how different forms of capital transform and reproduce each other. I cite here some works that I have found deeply helpful in understanding some of the concepts he has laid. See P. Bourdieu, (1973b), 'Cultural Reproduction and Social Reproduction', in R. Brown (ed.), *Knowledge, Education and Social Change*, London: Tavistock, (in French 1971); Also see J.D. Edgerton and L.W. Roberts, 'Cultural Capital or Habitus? Bourdieu and Beyond in the Explanation of Enduring Educational Inequality', *Theory and Research in Education*, *12*(2), (2014), pp. 193–220.

3   This is not a phenomenon exclusive to Chennai schools, this has been documented to happen in various educational settings across the world. Embodying privilege, schools becoming classificatory systems; bestowing ideas of giftedness has been well documented in literature on the sociology of education. For example, see Khan, Shamus Rahman, *Privilege: The Making of an Adolescent Elite at St. Paul's School* (Princeton University Press, 2021), and Van Zanten, Agnès, Stephen J. Ball, and Brigitte Darchy-Koechlin, eds. World Yearbook of Education 2015: Elites, Privilege and Excellence: The National and Global Redefinition of Educational Advantage (Routledge, 2015).

4   See P. Willis, *Learning to Labour: How Working-Class Kids Get Working Class Jobs*, (Routledge, 2017). I have broadly paraphrased the material presented from multiple pages in this book.

Chapter 7: Teaching History the 'Right' Way

1   hooks, bell, *Teaching to Transgress: Education as the Practice of Freedom* (New York; London: Routledge, 1994).

2   As quoted in Horton, Myles and Freire, Paulo. *We Make the Road by Walking: Conversations on Education and Social Change* (Temple University Press, 1990), p. 180.

3   In 'book cricket', students go to a random page of a large book (in this case, the textbook that was being read) and look at the last digit of the page on the right. So, if the page number is 43, then 3 runs have been scored, and the rules evolve with different students coming up with different variations.

4   For a detailed description of the events that led up to the Partition, see R. Guha, *India After Gandhi: The History of the World's Largest Democracy* (Pan Macmillan, 2017).

5   'PM Dreams of Breakfast in Amritsar, Dinner in Kabul',
    PTI, 8 January 2007, https://www.rediff.com/news/2007/
    jan/08pm.htm.

6   See R. Thapar, 'The History Debate and School Textbooks
    in India', *History Workshop Journal,* 67(1), (2009), pp. 87–98,
    https://doi.org/10.1093/hwj/dbn054.

7   As mentioned in N. Bhattacharya, 'Teaching History in
    Schools', *History Workshop Journal,* 67(1), (2009), pp. 99–110,
    https://doi.org/10.1093/hwj/dbn050.

8   See R. Thapar, 'The History Debate and School Textbooks in
    India'.

9   Ibid.

10 See N. Bhattacharya, 'Teaching History in Schools', *History
    Workshop Journal,* 67(1), (2009), pp. 99–110. https://doi.
    org/10.1093/hwj/dbn050.

11 M. Hasan, 'Textbooks and Imagined History: The BJP's
    Intellectual Agenda', *India International Centre Quarterly,* 29(1),
    (2002), pp. 75–90, http://www.jstor.org/stable/23005798.
    Also see https://thewire.in/history/ncert-history-textbooks-
    mughals-india#:~:text=The%20BJP%20government%20
    in%201999,was%20voted%20out%20in%202004.

12 See Bazmai, K., 'Union HRD minister Arjun Singh Appoints
    Committee to Review NCERT Textbooks', *India Today,* 9
    December 2011, https://www.indiatoday.in/magazine/
    education/story/20040705-arjun-singh-appoints-panel-to-
    review-ncert-textbooks-790544-2004-07-04.

13 See Balaji, 'Scholars Quit Textbook Body as Government
    Bans 1949 Cartoon', *The Hindu,* 16 November 2021, https://
    www.thehindu.com/news/national/scholars-quit-textbook-
    body-as-government-bans-1949-cartoon/article3409271.ece.

14 See P. Seixas, 'Schweigen! Die Kinder! or Does Postmodern
    History Have a Place in the Schools?' in P. Stearns, P. Seixas

and S.S. Wineburg, (eds.), *Knowing, Teaching and Learning History: National and International Perspectives* (New York: New York University Press, 2000). I have broadly paraphrased the material presented from multiple pages in this book.

15 See K. Sharma, 'History Textbooks Should Include 4 Vedas, Look at Post-1947 Events Too; House Panel Tells Govt.', ThePrint, 30 November 2021, https://theprint.in/india/ education/history-textbooks-should-include-4-vedas-look-at-post-1947-events-too-house-panel-tells-govt/774390/. An analysis of The Standing Committee on Education, Women, Children, Youth, and Sports (Chair: Dr Vinay P. Sahasrabuddhe) on *Reforms in Content and Design of School Text Books* can be found here: https://prsindia.org/policy/report-summaries/reforms-in-content-and-design-of-school-text-books.

16 For removal of references relating to the 2002 Gujarat riots, see https://nhrc.nic.in/sites/default/files/2023-4-06.pdf. See the same source for removing content relating to the Mughals.

17 See page 56 of https://ncert.nic.in/pdf/BookletClass11.pdf.

18 https://www.theguardian.com/world/2023/apr/06/indian-government-accused-of-rewriting-history-after-edits-to-schoolbooks.

19 This has been widely reported in the Indian media. See *The Hindu*'s coverage on this https://www.thehindu. com/education/ncert-drops-chapters-on-periodic-table-democracy-political-parties-from-class-10-syllabus/ article66919444.ece. For a complete list of all the topics that were dropped under the guise of 'syllabus rationalization', see https://ncert.nic.in/rationalised-content.php.

20 See C. Jaffrelot, *Modi's India: Hindu Nationalism and the Rise of Ethnic Democracy* (Princeton University Press, 2021). For a shorter excerpt on the topic of revising history curricula, see https://scroll.in/article/1010670/christophe-jaffrelot-on-the-way-hindutva-is-changing-history-and-science-

textbooks-in-schools. I have broadly paraphrased the material presented from multiple pages in this article.

21 See Korostelina, 'War of Textbooks: History Education in Russia and Ukraine', *Communist and Post-Communist Studies*, 43(2), (2010), pp. 129–37.

Conclusion: Who Deserves What?

1 See the table 'C-08: Educational Level by Age and Sex for Population Age 7 and Above (Total)', https://censusindia. gov.in/census.website/data/census-tables. Also see: Data from the census on total number of graduates in India as found in 'Only 8.15% of Indians Are Graduates, Census Data Show', 3 August 2015, *The Hindu*, https://www. thehindu.com/news/national/Only-8.15-of-Indians-are-graduates-Census-data-show/article60334841.ece.

2 See R.D. Lakes and P.A. Carter, 'Neoliberalism and Education: An Introduction', *Educational Studies (Ames)*, 47(2), (2011), pp. 107–10; Also see B. Davies and P. Bansel, 'Neoliberalism and Education', *International Journal of Qualitative Studies in Education*, 20(3), (2007), pp. 24–259.

3 See G. Adams, S. Estrada-Villalta, D. Sullivan, and H.R. Markus, 'The Psychology of Neoliberalism and the Neoliberalism of Psychology', *Journal of Social Issues*, 75(1), (2019), pp. 189–216.

4 See B. Davies and P. Bansel, 'Neoliberalism and Education', *International Journal of Qualitative Studies in Education*, 20(3), (2007), pp. 247–59.

5 M. Baas, 'Muscular India: Masculinity, Mobility and the New Middle Class', Context (New Delhi, 2020). Also see M. Baas, 'Muscles, Masculinity and Middle Classness', *Routledge Handbook of Contemporary India*, 444, 2016.

6 L. Fernandes, *India's New Middle Class: Democratic Politics in an Era of Economic Reform* (Minneapolis: University of Minnesota

Press, 2006). I have broadly paraphrased the material presented from multiple pages in this book.

7   A. Baviskar and R. Ray, (eds.). *Elite and Everyman: The Cultural Politics of the Indian Middle Classes* (Taylor & Francis, 2020).

8   H. Kharas, 'The Unprecedented Expansion of the Global Middle Class', (2019), p. 13, https://www.brookings.edu/wp-content/uploads/2017/02/global_20170228_global-middle-class.pdf.

9   C. Meyer, and N. Birdsall, 'New Estimates of India's Middle Class: A Technical Note', Centre for Global Development, November 2012, https://www.cgdev.org/sites/default/files/archive/doc/2013_MiddleClassIndia_TechnicalNote_CGDNote.pdf.

10 See R. Shukla, *How India Earns, Spends and Saves: Unmasking the Real India* (1st ed. New Delhi: SAGE Publications India Pvt. Ltd, 2010).

11 See Chapter 5 of S. Rukmini, *Whole Numbers and Half Truths: What Data Can and Cannot Tell Us About Modern India*, (2021). I have broadly paraphrased the material presented in multiple pages of this book.

12 'Learning Poverty Is a Combined Measure of Schooling and Learning', World Bank, https://www.worldbank.org/en/topic/education/brief/what-is-learning-poverty.

13 See the Statistical Appendix of the Economic Survey of India, www.indiabudget.gov.in/economicsurvey/doc/stat/tab83.pdf.

14 'Annual Status of Education Report (Rural) 2022', January 2023, Retrieved from https://img.asercentre.org/docs/ASER%202022%20report%20pdfs/All%20India%20documents/aserreport2022.pdf.

15 Madhav Chavan, Rukmini Banerjee's commentary can be found on page 15 of the ASER document. See Madhav Chavan's article titled 'Something is Changing' from the report:

https://img.asercentre.org/docs/ASER%202018/Release%20
Material/Articles/madhavchavansomethingischanging.pdf.

16 An analysis of learning outcome trends by ASER can be
found on their website: https://asercentre.org/trends-over-
time-reports/.

17 See here for the entire report on private schools in India:
Central Square Foundation, 'State of the Sector
Report on Private Schools in India', 2020, https://
centralsquarefoundation.org/State-of-the-Sector-Report-on-
Private-Schools-in-India.pdf.
It is important to read this report with the context that private
schools were surveyed before the COVID-19 pandemic. It
has been documented separately that after the pandemic,
there was an influx in public schools again. Nevertheless, the
allure and importance of private schooling as a structure and
institution remains. I have broadly paraphrased the material
presented from multiple pages in this report.

18 Ibid., p. 12 and p. 66

19 Ibid., p. 40.

20 Z. Bauman, *Wasted Lives: Modernity and Its Outcasts* (John Wiley
& Sons, 2013), p. 5.

21 T. Nagel, 'Equal Treatment and Compensatory
Discrimination', *Philosophy & Public Affairs*, (1973), pp. 348–63.